D1126523

Count Folke Bernadotte

THE CURTAIN FALLS

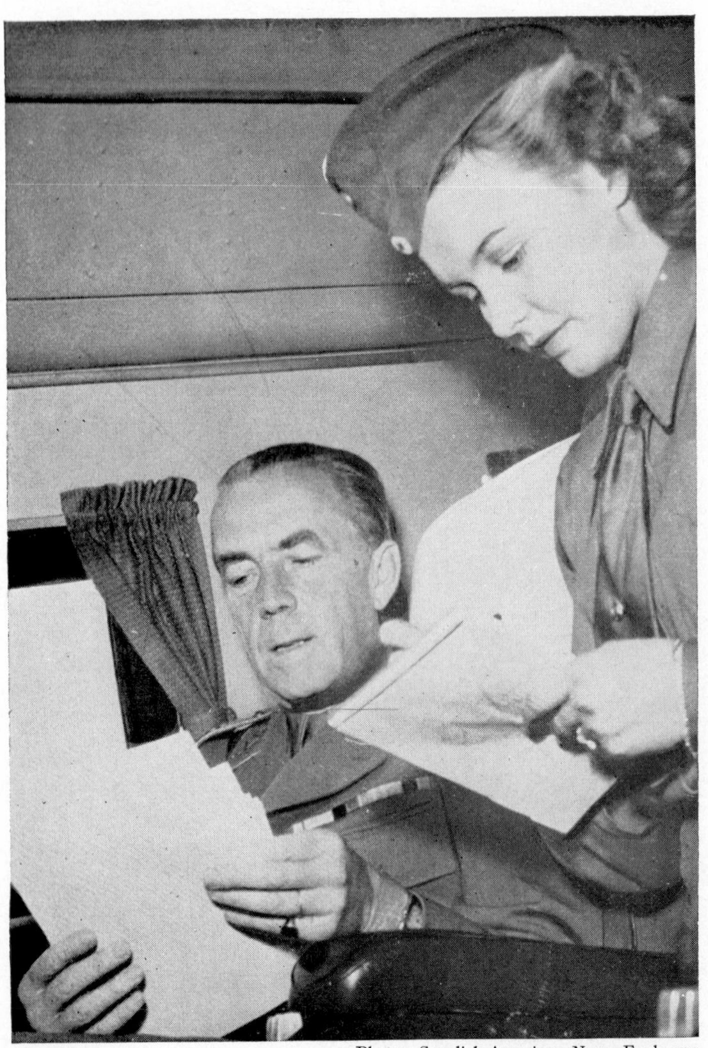

Photo—Swedish-American News Exchange

The Author dictating to his Swedish Red Cross secretary on one of his journeys by plane

Count Folke Bernadotte

THE CURTAIN FALLS

Last Days of the Third Reich

Translated from the Swedish by
Count Eric Lewenhaupt

New York / Alfred A. Knopf
1945

Manufactured in the United States of America.

FIRST AMERICAN EDITION

CONTENTS

ILLUSTRATIONS

PREFACE

It is with much hesitation that, after many requests, I have written an account of my experiences during my work in connection with the activity of the Swedish Red Cross in Germany in the last months of the second World War. I have overcome my hesitation in the hope that what I have told may throw some light on the dramatic events at the time of the collapse of the Third Reich.

The account is based on my notes and reports during my travels in Germany from the middle of February to the end of April of this year.

Stockholm, June 1945

The Author.

PARIS

November 1944

My plane left Bromma airfield, heading west, one day at the end of October 1944. My destination was Paris, via London. In Paris I was to confer with Allied representatives regarding Sweden's share in post-war reconstruction and other problems. Paris was again a free city in a free land, and even at that period one could safely prophesy that the life of the Nazi empire would be, not a thousand years, but little more than a decade.

There are two episodes of my visit to Paris that I shall always recollect with especial pleasure. One was my meeting with General Eisenhower, the other a luncheon at which the Swedish Consul General in Paris, Raoul Nordling, was one of the guests.

On a lovely autumn day, October 2nd, my plane landed on a military airfield at Versailles, where the Allied G.H.Q. had been established. I was immediately conducted to the Supreme Commander's office, where the General, a powerfully built man in his fifties, received me with the unaffected friendliness and absence of side that are characteristic of Americans in high positions.

I had been in charge of the organization concerned with the internment of American airmen who had made forced landings in Sweden, and it was on the suggestion of General Curtis of the United States Air Force, who had been to Sweden in connection with this matter, that I visited the Supreme Commander.

General Eisenhower impressed me enormously. I felt that here was a man of real greatness, a personality as vital as he was generous and warmhearted. He made one feel that he was relaxed and calm, that he had complete confidence in his ability to reach his goal and carry out the gigantic task he had undertaken. Here, I felt, was a man who knew what he wanted and had the ability to get it. One of his most striking characteristics was his strong sense of humor. It was seldom absent during our talk, and it gave a charmingly human touch to his personality. The General is very human, and very humane. He expressed no hate for those who had been his antagonists in the second World War, and certainly none for the enemy's military leaders.

His subordinates are unanimous as to the complete absence of any military rigidity in their Supreme Commander. This characteristic is perhaps the explanation of his greatest quality: the magnificent ability with which he has preserved the team spirit among the Western Allies and, often under conditions of great delicacy, adjusted and co-ordinated the sometimes conflicting wishes expressed from various quarters.

General Eisenhower began his talk by expressing his appreciation of what I had been able to do for American airmen in Sweden, and then went on to discuss the general situation. I noted particularly that he seemed to have a friendly understanding of Sweden's political attitude. In any event, he stated in the course of this talk that he was of the firm opinion that Sweden's neutral policy had been the right one, not only from her own point of view, but also from that of the Allies. This was an opinion that I encountered during several of my conversations with representatives of the British and American High Commands.

General Eisenhower then discussed with me the question of how and where Sweden could most effectively assist in the post-war problems. I informed him that I had had a preliminary discussion with representatives of UNRRA, and that the Swedish authorities and the Swedish Red Cross were anxious to hear the views of SHAEF. I mentioned that in certain quarters of UNRRA doubts had been expressed whether the offers of assistance by neutrals would be favorably received. Eisenhower strongly rejected this view and declared that all the assistance offered would be needed. Personally, he said, he thought it very natural that neutral countries should wish to take part in the task of restoration. He wished the occupied countries to establish their own administrations as soon as they were liberated, after which they would be regarded and treated as sovereign states with which neutral organizations could deal direct and plan post-war action.

Regarding Germany, General Eisenhower stated that the Allied Supreme Headquarters would collaborate only with a single organization covering all the zones of occupation. When I asked him for his opinion concerning Poland in this connection, he expressed the opinion that it would be only right if, for example, the Swedish Red Cross approached the Polish authorities to ascertain their wishes, but that the Russian authorities would probably expect to be consulted. He emphasized, however, that he was not in possession of detailed information regarding plans in Eastern Europe.

I was greatly struck by the atmosphere at Eisenhower's headquarters. It was gay and friendly, and there were many signs of the never-failing American sense of humor. When I was shown around I saw in a niche a bust of Göring that the Germans had forgotten in their precipitate flight. There it stood, but the face was turned towards the wall. "He's a bad boy," said my guide, laughing; "he must stand in the corner until he says he is ashamed of himself." Among those with whom I had lengthy talks was General Spaatz, chief of the Allied Strategic Air Forces. One of his remarks impressed itself on me: "Sometimes when I lie awake at night and think about the appalling destruction my forces cause in Germany and among the civilian population, I have to force myself to dwell on the suffering the French people have undergone at the hands of the Germans. Only that thought makes it a little less painful to deal such blows at innocent people in Germany." General Spaatz said that he had never observed any hatred for the enemy in either the American or the British forces.

In one of the rooms at Supreme Headquarters I noticed a map on which were indicated the various zones of occupation in Germany as planned at that period of the war. There were three main zones. One line, following the course of the Elbe from Lübeck to the east, showed the western boundary of the planned Russian zone. Northwestern Germany was to be under British occupation, and the Southwest under the Americans. I felt, however, that here was no concern of mine, and I refrained from asking any questions. I had come to Paris to discuss details connected with Sweden's humanitarian mission and for no political purpose.

The following day, November 3rd, I attended a luncheon given at the Hotel Bristol by the Swedish Chargé d'Affaires, K. A. Belfrage. Among those present were my two traveling companions, Doctor Ulf Nordwall, medical adviser on post-war problems to the Swedish Red Cross, and Baron Erik Leijonhufuud, secretary to the Swedish Government Committee for International Relief. In addition there was our Consul General Raoul Nordling. I must admit that this man fascinated me. His enthusiasm was as irresistible as it was inspiring. I had, of course, read in the papers about Nordling's magnificent contribution to the liberation of Paris. I knew that he had played a highly important part as negotiator between the Allied forces and the French underground movement on the one hand, and the German occupational authorities on the other. Nordling is an old Parisian Swede filled with a deep love of France and the French and a passionate desire to be of help to the vast number who so heroically carried on the struggle for their country's freedom. His activities were sometimes misunderstood. It was necessary to maintain contact with the enemy as well as with the underground movement, and this necessity gave rise to suspicions that have since shown themselves to be entirely without foundation. As we sat over our luncheon he told us in a frank and vivacious way of his many adventures and experiences during the days preceding the liberation of Paris. What especially interested and thrilled me was his account of how he had been able to prevent large numbers of women and men from being deported to Germany, and how he had succeeded in persuading the Germans to release a number of Frenchmen who had been imprisoned in France at the time of the capitulation of Paris. Nordling is not a civil servant who fears responsibility and takes cover under regulations and instructions. Rather, he acts fearlessly on his own responsibility. Without this trait he could never have succeeded in his self-imposed mission. As I listened to him I became infected by his enthusiasm. I asked myself if I couldn't do something similar for those who were languishing in German concentration camps. Thus was sown in me a seed that was to develop into the Swedish Red Cross expedition to Germany in the spring of 1945.

STOCKHOLM

New Year 1944–5

In the plane that was carrying me home my mind was occupied with the project to which Raoul Nordling's talk had given rise. Would it be possible for Sweden to do something to lessen the suffering caused by the German system of concentration camps—to save at least some of the unfortunates otherwise doomed to die in horrible conditions? I felt little optimism, for I was well aware that the German authorities had firmly rejected all suggestions, whether they came from the international or national Red Cross organizations, neutrals included, that Red Cross activity be extended to the concentration camps. The Germans absolutely declined to allow any foreigner a glimpse into these hells, as we feared them to be. Nor could we refer to any international agreement, for when the Geneva Convention was drawn up in 1929 nobody had as yet thought of incarcerating civilian political prisoners in concentration camps. It was reserved for Nazi Germany to conceive and apply this diabolical device. The concentration camps were well guarded. No one forced behind those grim walls could escape, and no independent observer could enter, lest the dark secrets of the grim system be publicly disclosed. Of one thing I was convinced: it would be useless to negotiate with any but the most highly placed in the Nazi hierarchy. I knew that if anything was to be done, it must be done without delay. For some time there had been rumors, impossible to ignore, that the German authorities meant to liquidate the prisoners in concentration camps if there should be a collapse in Germany's defenses, and thus to rid themselves of dangerous witnesses.

These were my thoughts on my return to Stockholm. And, as in Paris, it was an encounter with a single person that proved to be of decisive importance to the execution of my scheme. This time it was a distinguished Norwegian diplomat,

Mr. Niels Christian Ditleff, a man of sixty who had served his country in many important posts and was at this time attached to the Norwegian Legation in Stockholm. It was he who suggested to me that the most important achievement in sight would be to persuade the Nazi authorities to let Norwegian civilians be released from the camps in Germany and evacuated to Sweden. The idea appealed to me greatly, for it was very similar to what Consul General Nordling was doing, though perhaps on a larger scale. Mr. Ditleff and I went deeply into the question, and we arrived at the conclusion that to be successful it would be necessary to get access to the head of the SS, Reichsführer Heinrich Himmler. In such matters final decision rested with him. A somewhat encouraging factor was that he was known to have expressed a liking for the Scandinavian countries and their peoples. There was perhaps a faint hope that he might give his approval.

The next move was to confer with the Swedish Red Cross and with the Swedish Government. I knew that the latter had long been trying to do something for the Scandinavians imprisoned in

Germany. Many requests for the liberation of individual prisoners had been made through our legation in Berlin. The Swedish Minister, Arvid Richert, had been untiring in his efforts, which had been by no means fruitless. He had, for instance, succeeded in obtaining the release of a number of Norwegian students who had been returned to Norway. This fact was brought up during the ensuing discussions in January and the beginning of February, at which it was agreed that it was far more difficult for a diplomatic representative than for a private individual to make contact with those in authority over the concentration camps. As a diplomat he could attempt such approach only through the channels of the Ministry of Foreign Affairs, and there was always the risk that it would get stuck there and never reach Himmler, who had the final decision in matters affecting the concentration camps. When the Swedish Foreign Office instructed me to make an attempt to obtain the release of Norwegian civilians, a plan was agreed on.

At the request of the Swedish Minister, Richert, the Red Cross had sent an expedition to Berlin at the beginning of February—that is, while my discussions were taking place. The object of the expedition was to collect and send home the numerous Swedish-born women who had married Germans and now found themselves homeless and with no near relations. This gave me an excellent pretext for a visit to Berlin. On my departure by plane on February 16th it was officially announced that I was going to inspect the Red Cross expedition to ascertain if it required reinforcing in order to carry out its task. The real object of my visit was, of course, to try to meet Himmler and get his consent to the internment in Sweden, not only of the Norwegian, but also of the Danish prisoners in Germany. Before my departure I had submitted my plans not only to the Swedish Government, but also to the President of the Swedish Red Cross, Prince Karl. He had expressed the opinion that the scheme must embrace Danes as well as Norwegians. The field of operations had thus been considerably widened.

BERLIN

February 1945

I had no illusions as to the difficulties of my task, and little hope of obtaining more than a partial success. Though well aware of the many obstacles in my path, I nevertheless persuaded myself that if I could only meet Himmler I could not fail to obtain some concession. The difficulty was just how to reach this man, at that time believed to be the most powerful personage in Germany. He was then commanding the German armies on the Oder front, and as the Russian pressure on them was very great, his presence on this front was indispensable. My difficulties were not diminished by the fact that I could not give the real reason for my visit to those on whose help I was counting to bring about a meeting. It would have been much too easy for them to put a stop to the whole undertaking if they disapproved of the project.

When I arrived in Berlin the Yalta Conference had just ended, and according to the communiqué issued by Churchill, Roosevelt, and Stalin the Allies were now going to co-ordinate their forces and launch a simultaneous attack on Germany from east, west, north, and south. The Russians had already obtained a foothold on Reich territory, and in the west the British and Americans were preparing their great Rhine offensive. But though the Third Reich was beginning to crumble, the Germans continued their policy of terror in the occupied territories. Between February 8th and 10th no fewer than thirty-four patriots had been murdered by the Germans in Norway. Events were rushing with increasing speed toward the last great crisis, when anything might happen.

Berlin seemed war-weary. The people looked fairly well fed, and though there were long queues outside food shops, in the end customers apparently got what they wanted. There was no real shortage of food, but people gave the impression of being utterly sick of the war and completely dominated by the wish to see it end quickly. The erection of barricades in the streets had begun. There was no panic, but neither was there any enthusiasm. The citizens of the Third Reich worked with that mechanical sense of duty which is characteristic of the German. The men mostly belonged to the Volkssturm, but there were women as well—labor service was universal—and naturally there were a good many foreign workers from the concentration camps. On closer inspection the barricades looked very flimsy. Anything that happened to be handy was used; busses, streetcars, and motor cars were placed in position and filled with bricks and rubble. If the work proceeded without much enthusiasm, the Berliners had not lost their caustic sense of humor. One of the jokes of that time was that when the Russians came to Berlin it would take them one hour and two minutes to capture each barricade: one hour for Homeric laughter, and the remaining two minutes to overcome the obstacle.

At the barricades and in food queues the Berliners were waiting for the enemy's arrival, while around them in all directions death and destruction increased day by day. In the central parts of the city four houses out of every five appeared to have been destroyed by the terrific bombardments. Many of the inhabitants had, of course, been evacuated, but people continued to live in cellars, and if things were not exactly at their best, life still went on fairly normally. The underground railways, as well as gas, electricity, and telephones, ceased functioning during air raids.

One wondered what the people thought of the general situation; what thoughts were hidden behind their dull, apathetic faces. It is certain, however, that their faith in the Nazi system had been severely shaken, and that, despite Doctor Goebbels's pep talks, the belief was general that Germany had lost the war. Very characteristically, there was often an inability, or perhaps I should say disinclination, to realize that the blame for the whole disaster rested with Hitler. A large part of the population clung sentimentally to their Führer right up to the end. They felt their oath of allegiance binding upon them. Adolf Hitler's fantastic dreams, which to other nations were nightmares, had become the Germans' wishful thinking. They could not bear to lose their faith in him who had appeared to them as a redeemer. Nor could they give up their belief in the justification of the Hitler program.

The Chief of the Security Police, Obergruppenführer Ernst Kaltenbrunner, was courteous enough as he offered me Chesterfield cigarettes and Dubonnet—doubtless looted from France—but the eyes that he fixed on me were cold and inquisitorial. The meeting, which had been arranged by the Swedish Legation, took place at Kaltenbrunner's luxurious home at Wannsee on the day following my arrival in Berlin. My immediate object was to convince Kaltenbrunner, Himmler's second-in-command in the Gestapo, that it was imperative for me to meet his chief.

Obergruppenführer Kaltenbrunner could look back with pride upon a distinguished career, and he had earned the well-merited confidence of his superiors, for he had always shown zeal and efficiency. He had quickly risen to be chief of the Gestapo in Vienna. When the notorious Heydrich, the appointed Reich Protector of Bohemia and Moravia, was murdered, after having himself murdered an unknown number of Czech patriots, Kaltenbrunner was his obvious successor as chief of the Gestapo. Not only had nature provided him with the necessary abilities, but in appearance he was all that one would expect a Gestapo chief to be. It was fairly obvious that Obergruppenführer Kaltenbrunner could have little understanding of any humanitarian proposal in connection with the German concentration camps.

At our meeting he was polite, cool, and inquisitive. He was anxious to know why I wished to see Himmler. As he sipped his Dubonnet he pointed out how extremely difficult it was to arrange a meeting. He suggested that instead I should explain my purposes to him, whereupon he would transmit them to his chief. This alternative was, of course, quite unacceptable to me. It was therefore necessary to get him sufficiently interested in arranging a meeting with Himmler, and to do it without giving away the real object of my visit. According to my notes, our conversation proceeded roughly as follows:

Bernadotte: "As you are doubtless aware, relations between Sweden and Germany are extremely bad. Swedish public opinion is intensely anti-German. This is principally because of German cruelty in Norway and Denmark, the scorched-earth policy in North Norway, and above all the taking of hostages. German methods in these countries are often in flagrant violation of international conventions. Reichsminister Himmler occupies a position that would make it possible for him to adopt measures calculated to improve Swedish-German relations. As I understand the situation, this would be principally in Germany's interest."

Kaltenbrunner: "Are you acting under official instructions?"

Bernadotte: "No, but I can assure you that not only the Swedish Government, but the whole Swedish people, share the opinion I have just indicated."

Kaltenbrunner: "I am well aware that the relations between our two countries are most unsatisfactory, and I deplore it. I also know that Reichsminister Himmler is particularly anxious to bring about good relations between Germany and Sweden. But I must point out that the taking of hostages has proved necessary in the fight against sabotage. Similar measures have been taken by the Russians without Swedish public opinion being roused."

Bernadotte: "It seems to me that it should be of great importance for Germany not to make an enemy of Sweden, whether Germany wins the war or not."

At this point the third person present at the meeting joined in the conversation. It was Brigadeführer[1] Walter Schellenberg. He remarked: "It would be a great misfortune for Germany if Sweden were to be dragged into the war against her."

Schellenberg, a man of about thirty-five, gave me the impression of being the very antithesis of Kaltenbrunner. A lawyer by profession, in 1940 he had been appointed chief of the Political Section of the German Intelligence Service, and in 1944 head of the whole organization. In this

[1] Brigadeführer is a Nazi Party or SS rank roughly parallel with that of an Army Major General. TRANSLATOR

capacity he played a very important part, especially because, I gathered, he had worked energetically to bring about a change in the policy of the Third Reich, its foreign policy especially. He had, moreover, tried to combat the bestialities of the Gestapo. During my ensuing long and confidential talks with him he told me that Kaltenbrunner hated him and had even tried, though without success, to make Himmler believe that he was in the pay of the British Secret Service. I am quite willing to admit that from the first I felt a certain confidence in Schellenberg, and in any case I shall always be grateful to him for the valuable help he gave me in connection with my Red Cross work in Germany.

As the discussion went on, Kaltenbrunner did his best to pump me about my proposals to Himmler and asked if I had any concrete suggestions. I said that I had not, and generally tried to avoid going too deeply into matters with him, for if he were to disapprove of my objectives, he could easily wreck my hopes of meeting his chief. I told him, however, that there were two principal concessions I wanted. One was the issue of exit permits to Swedish women married to Germans, and to their children, particularly women whose homes had been bombed or whose husbands were killed or missing. The other was permission to the Swedish Red Cross to work in the internment camps in Germany. Oddly enough, Kaltenbrunner showed himself reasonable and understanding on these points, and I asked him if he now saw how important it was that I should see Himmler personally, even though a favorable reply to these requests would not be enough to bring about a change in Swedish public opinion. Kaltenbrunner assured me emphatically that he quite agreed. When I left him I felt that I had made good progress and had reason to be hopeful about my chances of a talk with Himmler.

The Reichsminister for Foreign Affairs, Joachim von Ribbentrop, received me at the Foreign Office. This building had been bombed, though the rooms in which I was received appeared undamaged. Ribbentrop seemed to be in excellent form and filled with the consciousness

Count Schwerin von Krosigk
Foreign Minister in the Dönitz cabinet

Grand Admiral Karl Dönitz

of his own importance and dignity. He invited me to be seated by the fire and immediately plunged into a speech. I surreptitiously set my stop watch.

I should mention here that only a few hours after my arrival in Berlin it was reported to me that the German Foreign Office was displaying the greatest interest in my visit and was particularly anxious to know the reasons for my wishing to meet Himmler. It was no secret that the relations between Herr von Ribbentrop and the head of the Gestapo were decidedly cool. While I was dining in the temporary quarters of the Swedish Legation in the Rauchstrasse—very near the old Legation, which had been completely destroyed in a recent air raid—a message from Ribbentrop reached me, expressing the wish to see me at the Foreign Office the following day. In consequence I drove straight there from Obergruppenführer Kaltenbrunner's residence.

—I stopped my stop watch. It indicated that the Minister for Foreign Affairs had talked for one hour and seven minutes without my being given an opportunity to get in a word. Again using my notes, I reproduce fairly exactly the tenor of his talk:

After having expressed, in the warmest and most flattering terms, his great appreciation of my contribution to the exchange of prisoners of war and to the work of the Swedish Red Cross in Holland and elsewhere, he threw himself into what I can only describe as an oration. It was delivered in a voice that at times trembled with emotion, at others resembled a roar suitable only to the tribune of a packed Kroll Opera House. In between these extremes, he commented on his own personal achievements with simulated humility. He began his address by explaining to me the differences between National Socialism and Bolshevism. In his view Hitler had succeeded in convincing the German workingman of the necessity of retaining the classes that make up society, though these had to be adapted to the Nazi ideology. Bolshevism, on the other hand, had taught that the privileged classes must be "liquidated." This, in Ribbentrop's opinion, was the fundamental difference between the two systems.

He thereupon proceeded to explain why it had been an absolute necessity for Germany to conclude a pact with the Soviet Union in 1939, and described certain conversations he had had with Stalin and Molotov. The reason why Ribbentrop had invited the Commissar for Foreign Affairs to Berlin was the growing suspicion of Russia and the desire to know exactly what her attitude was. One of the reasons for this suspicion was the fact that, on the occasion of certain trade negotiations, the Soviet had sent no fewer than nine hundred and sixty delegates. It was clear that the Russians had come for the purpose of spying out the land. Everything showed that war between Germany and Russia was inevitable; in fact, it was known that Russia had intended to attack Germany in August 1941. But what had made any further hesitation impossible was a conversation that Ribbentrop had had with Molotov during an air raid following a state banquet in honor of the Russian Commissar for Foreign Affairs. On this occasion they had been obliged to spend several hours in a shelter, and Molotov had made use of the occasion to insist on Germany's guaranteeing Russia certain bases on the Skagerrak and the Kattegat—a demand that Ribbentrop refused with equal firmness, primarily because he had no wish to see the Scandinavian countries exposed to the danger of bolshevization.

Should the German eastern front collapse, the whole of Europe was in grave danger of becoming bolshevized, Ribbentrop went on. He asserted that he knew all the details of Stalin's plans for Europe, which aimed at nothing less than the creation of a number of Soviet republics on the Continent. He went so far as to tell me the names of the individuals Stalin had chosen to be the leaders of these satellites of the Soviet Union. However, he diplomatically left out his own country and Scandinavia. He assured me that if Germany were to lose the war, Russian bombers would be over Stockholm within six months and that the Bolsheviks would shoot all the members of the Royal Family, myself included. From talks he had had with Stalin, he was also convinced that it was Russia's intention to subjugate, not only the whole of Europe, but also India and China, and that therefore every bomb Churchill and Roosevelt dropped on Germany was another nail in the coffins of the British Empire and the U.S.A. He told me he was at that very time making a last attempt, through special channels, to convince the governments of the Anglo-Saxon countries of the fate that awaited Europe if Germany were to collapse, and he was going to appeal to Churchill and Roosevelt to stop the offensive in the west and to cease bombing German cities. He added that he had very little hope of success.

After that Ribbentrop reversed himself and with obvious lack of logic declared that it would be more advantageous to Germany if Russia occupied the European continent, rather than the Western Allies. He went on to say that if the German High Command should decide that the line of the Oder could no longer be held, they would prefer to "throw themselves into the arms of Russia" and transfer a number of divisions to the west, rather than surrender to England and America. If the line of the Oder cracked, it was a sign that Fate had decided that Europe should be bolshevized. That would, he maintained, happen in any case, even if western and central Germany were occupied by British and American armies, for Stalin, after a short period, would insist on their being replaced by Russians.

Subsequent talks that I had with a number of leading Germans confirmed that Ribbentrop belonged to that school of German statesmen who advocated rapprochement with the Soviet Union. He was in favor of European domination by a strong Russia and an equally powerful Germany. Many of the Germans with whom I spoke expressed the fear that this school would gain the ascendancy. When this subject was discussed I always maintained that, even so, Stalin would never agree to a coalition that would automatically end his country's alliance with Britain and America.

Ribbentrop continued by saying that Hitler was the only one to have realized that the Continent would become bolshevized if Germany collapsed. It was an appalling tragedy that Britain and Germany should have gone to war against each other—the more so because this war could so easily have been prevented if Britain had not attacked Germany. He also deplored the blindness of the Finnish Government in making a separate peace with Russia, and predicted that Field Marshal Carl Gustaf Mannerheim would soon share the fate of the Rumanian and Bulgarian leaders. In other words, he would be shot.

Turning suddenly to the occupied countries, he said he was convinced that Germany had made a mistake in dealing too leniently with the populations of these countries. Then came the climax of his address. He posed a question. Whom, he asked, did I regard as the contemporary who had contributed the most to humanity? Without giving me time to reply he answered his own question: "Adolf Hitler. Unquestionably Adolf Hitler." Adolf Hitler, said Ribbentrop, was filled with the friendliest feelings for Sweden. And there was no one living, he added, whom he venerated as much as Sweden's monarch. Here at last I was able to get a word in. I told Ribbentrop, as I had told Kaltenbrunner, about the extremely hostile feeling against Germany among the Swedish people. But this only gave Ribbentrop an opportunity to air his own rather original ideas. He said that this Swedish hostility was deplored in Germany, but that he personally was quite unable to understand it. He thought it a great advantage to Sweden that there were German troops in Norway, for if there were not, the English would certainly have occupied that country, and they would not have shown the respect for Sweden's frontiers that Germany had shown.

Before I went, Ribbentrop asked me if I had any concrete proposals calculated to improve the relations between the two countries, to which I replied that I hoped the Swedish Red Cross would be allowed to carry out certain work in the concentration camps, and that this concession would make a favorable impression in Sweden. I had no intention of letting him know my real objectives. Ribbentrop approved of my scheme and said he was glad I was going to meet Himmler. I suggested that we should have another talk after that meeting, and this was agreed upon.

Someone once—not very recently—called Herr von Ribbentrop the Bismarck of the twentieth century. It is unquestionably a fact that, in his way, he has continued the work of the Iron Chancellor, but it is equally true that in the end he contributed enormously to rendering it void. Nor can it be denied that he stamped the foreign policy of the Third Reich with his own personality from that day in 1938 when he was installed in the Wilhelmstrasse. He triumphed in Munich in 1938 and the following year in Prague. But his greatest triumph was in Moscow in 1939, when he put his signature on the German-Russian pact. And now, in the spring of 1945, as I talked with him and a number of other Nazi bigwigs, I had the impression that he still had Hitler's ear and enjoyed his support. Ribbentrop was the man who had shown the world what Germany was able to do in the field of foreign policy. It was evident that in Hitler's eyes Ribbentrop was a man who had earned the gratitude of his country.

Sitting with him in his room in the Auswärtiges Amt and listening to his long-winded speech, which reminded me of a somewhat worn phonograph record, I reflected that here was a man of very small mental stature and, moreover, rather ridiculous. It was an astonishing thought that this man had all these years been Minister for Foreign Affairs of the German Reich. But obviously he now realized that the game was lost, though he occasionally assured one of the very opposite. He believed that he had the solution to the problems that were piling up higher and higher in the path of Germany and in his own path. He would repeat the famous coup of 1939 when he made the pact with Russia. He would find a new road to Moscow. It was plain to me that this was in his mind when I left him that February night to go to my car, which was waiting for me in the Wilhelmstrasse.

HOHEN-LÜCHEN

February 1945

My hopes were not to be disappointed. My request for a meeting with Himmler had been granted, and at five o'clock on the afternoon of February 12th I was fetched by Schellenberg and driven with him to Hohen-Lüchen, a large hospital seventy-five miles from Berlin in a northerly direction. The head physician, Professor Gebhart, himself down with pneumonia, received me in his sickroom and gave me some data about his establishment. It was filled to the last bed, he said. Among the German refugees in it were numerous children, about eighty of whom had had to have amputations because of frostbite and bullet wounds. It was a grim picture the Professor presented to me, and it was against this background that I was to meet Heinrich Himmler, supreme head of the SS, the Gestapo, the whole German police system, Minister of the Interior, and Commander-in-Chief of the home army—the man whose system of terrorization had stained politics with crime in a manner hitherto unknown, and who, by means of this very system, had up to this moment held the tottering Third Reich upright.

William Shirer, in his *Berlin Diary*, describes Himmler as a quiet little man who looks like a harmless country schoolmaster—an excellent superficial description of the Gestapo chief. When I suddenly saw him before me in the green Waffenschutzstaffel uniform, without any decorations and wearing horn-rimmed spectacles, he looked a typical unimportant official, and one would certainly have passed him in the street without noticing him. He had small, well-shaped and delicate hands, and they were carefully manicured, although this was forbidden in the SS. He was, to my great surprise, extremely affable. He gave evidence of a sense of humor, tending rather to the macabre. Frequently he introduced a joke when conversation was threatening to become awkward or heavy. Certainly there was nothing diabolical in his appearance. Nor did I observe any sign of that icy hardness in his expression of which I had heard so much.

Himmler in his talks with me seemed a very vivacious personality, inclined to sentimentality where his relations with the Führer were concerned, and with a great capacity for enthusiasm. It was a most extraordinary experience to hear this man, who had sent millions of human beings to their death by the most monstrous methods, speak with enthusiasm of the chivalrous manner in which the English and the Germans had waged war in France in the summer of 1944, on occasion interrupting actions in order that each might gather up their wounded.

A Norwegian who had worked among Norwegian prisoners of war in Germany had told me that Himmler took a deep interest in Scandinavian runic inscriptions, and at the end of our talk I presented him with a Swedish seventeenth-century work on this subject. Himmler seemed noticeably affected; he told me that he was deeply touched and grateful that I should have thought of giving him this pleasure as conditions stood. He had at one time used his influence on behalf of Professor

Didrik Seip, Rector of the University of Oslo and one of the most heroic figures among the Norwegian patriots. Was this intervention due to concern about the fate he knew awaited him, was it sentimentality, or did it mean admiration for a man who dared speak his mind fearlessly? Whatever the explanation may be, Himmler was certainly one of the most contradictory characters I have ever encountered. The experiences of Professor Seip and of Bishop Eivind Berggrav, the two great Norwegian patriots, which they related to me, parallel my own observations and impressions. Himmler ordered Professor Seip to be released from the concentration camp where he had been held and, apologizing for the brutal manner in which he had been treated, offered him every facility for continuing his scientific studies in Germany, with the same remuneration he had received as Rector of the University of Oslo. Seip told me that he regarded Himmler as a kind of idealist, with a particular liking for the Scandinavian countries. And when I met Bishop Berggrav in Oslo, in the middle of May this year, he expressed a similar opinion. He told me that one day Himmler had visited him. Berggrav asked whether he wanted him to talk frankly or to say the kind of things Himmler would like to hear. Himmler told him he would be much interested to hear his honest opinion. After this talk Josef Terboven, Reich Commissar in Norway, had demanded Berggrav's execution, but the demand was vetoed by Himmler. Nothing, however, can exonerate Heinrich Himmler from the terrible guilt that was his; no extenuation, even, can be found for his conduct. He it was who created the concentration camp system, and even if, as he asserted, he was unaware of the horrible cruelties to which it gave rise, it was he who must bear the responsibility. When I talked to him he indicated in various ways that he knew this very well. He also showed that he was fully conscious of the immense difficulties of the situation in which he found himself—difficulties inherent partly in the military situation and partly in his relations with his Führer.

Every German would fight like a lion before he gave up hope, Himmler declared when I asked him if he didn't think it meaningless to go on with the war, since Germany could not possibly be victorious. Certainly the military situation was grave, very grave, but not hopeless. When he had taken over the command of the Oder front there was a breach of 350 kilometers in the line which invited a penetration by the Russians. He had had orders to close this breach, and he had succeeded in calling up fresh levies and even in bringing up troops from less exposed fronts. There was no immediate risk of a Russian break-through on the Oder front, Himmler declared.

It was probably the "inner front" that was Himmler's greatest headache. Obviously he was still in close contact with Hitler; in fact, he made that plain himself, emphasizing his unswerving devotion to the Führer. "You may think it sentimental, even absurd, but I have sworn loyalty to Adolf Hitler, and as a soldier and as a German I cannot go back on my oath. For that reason I cannot do anything in opposition to the Führer's plans and wishes."

It is almost certain that Hitler was in full control at that time. To some extent the actual leadership may have passed out of his hands, but it was easy to see that many of those nearest him continued to have great respect for him and did not dare oppose him. His influence was still enormous, although it was gradually becoming more and more negative: that is, he no longer initiated new measures, but merely vetoed those of his collaborators.

Shortly before my arrival in Germany the former President of the Swiss National Confederation, Jean Marie Musy, had come to an agreement with Himmler whereby the Jews interned in the concentration camp at Theresienstadt should be transported to Switzerland en route to the United States. The foreign press got wind of it and published the facts. This was reported to Hitler by one of his press observers, and Himmler was summoned to appear before the Führer. Asked what concessions Germany had obtained in exchange, Himmler replied that Germany had obtained nothing at all, whereupon Hitler had one of his seizures of rage and forbade any further transportations of this kind. Himmler had to accept this decision; the transportations ceased; and when Musy returned to Berlin he found it impossible to gain an interview with the Gestapo chief.

It was against this background that I began my work in Germany: Hitler raging because of the concession made, and Himmler not being able, not daring, or not caring to oppose his master. Schellenberg told me that at this period a certain strain in the relations between the Führer and the head of the Gestapo was noticeable. Himmler declared his unswerving loyalty. But his freedom of action was restricted.

"Is it your intention that the Norwegians and Danes now in German concentration camps whom you want sent to Sweden shall be given police training there? Do you really consider a country neutral when it does such things?" Himmler shot this at me sharply, and when I replied that I had nothing to do with these matters, he immediately went on: "If I were to agree to your proposals, the Swedish papers would announce with big headlines that the war criminal Himmler, in terror of punishment for his crimes, is trying to buy his freedom."

We had now reached the crucial point in our talk, which lasted two hours and a half, and at which Schellenberg was present. As was my practice, I had begun by pointing out the hostile feeling toward Germany in Sweden, whereupon Himmler at once counterattacked and produced a number of arguments to illustrate the innocence and humaneness of Germany's policy. The bad feeling, he said, was entirely chargeable to agitation in the Swedish press, in particular the *Göteborgs Handelstidningen.* It was the Allies who had begun the system of dropping saboteurs by parachute. It was since the Allied occupation, and not during the German occupation, that conditions had deteriorated so catastrophically in France, Holland, Italy, and Greece. It would have been easy enough for the Germans to have occupied the whole of France in 1941, but they had refrained from doing so. It was absolutely essential to act forcefully, in fact with the greatest ruthlessness, in places where the population had begun openly to fight the German troops.

Himmler offered excuses, justifications, and explanations for everything, but he also made an admission. When I asked him if he himself would not take up arms against the invader if he were a citizen of an occupied country, and if he did not think the Norwegian and Danish Fighters for Freedom were performing a patriotic and national duty, he replied in the affirmative. But, he hastened to add, saboteurs must be prepared to take the consequences of their acts. I answered by saying that it was not the punishment of saboteurs that had aroused such indignation in Sweden, but the device of taking hostages and the killing of so many innocent people, both contrary to humanitarian feeling and international opinion. Himmler denied these occurrences; whereupon I gave him a few definite instances. He said there could be no question but that I was misinformed. At a subsequent meeting he himself brought up an example I had cited and admitted that an inquiry he had instituted showed my facts to be correct. If this was a premeditated piece of acting, it was certainly well done. Then came the usual question: Had I any concrete proposals?

I asked him if it would not be better for him to suggest any measures that might improve the situation; to which he replied that he could suggest nothing. It was at this point that I made the proposal about the release of Norwegians and Danes for internment in Sweden, to which Himmler reacted so violently. In addition to what I have already reported he said that, whether or no, Sweden and the Allies would have to give some compensation for such a concession—e.g., an assurance that sabotage would cease in Norway.

The shadow of Hitler fell across the room at that moment. After the agreement with Musy, Hitler had at once asked what concession Germany had obtained. If Himmler came to terms with me, he would have the same question hurled at him again. It was evident that Himmler's hands were tied; that he was not so powerful as many believed. The Führer was alive, and, for one reason or another, he could not be ignored.

I told Himmler that the concession he had mentioned was quite unthinkable.

I had met with an uncompromising refusal, but the bargaining was not over. I changed the topic by saying that the Swedish Red Cross was very anxious for permission to work in the concentration camps, especially in those where Norwegians and Danes were interned.

Himmler: "That would probably be very useful, and I see no reason why permission should not be granted."

Bernadotte: "And to facilitate the work, the Norwegians and Danes in question should be collected into two camps, one for each group. The total number of Norwegian and Danish prisoners is probably somewhere about thirteen thousand."

Himmler: "That figure is greatly exaggerated. I don't know the exact number, but I should not think it can be more than two or three thousand. However, I shall look into the matter."

Himmler had accepted my proposal. He also agreed that the aged, the sick, and mothers should be allowed to return to Norway after having been assembled in the camps. He did not even raise any objection to the Swedish Red Cross staffs being admitted to the camps to assist in the collection of the prisoners.

There remained one subject, a delicate as well as an important one. It concerned the Swedish women who had married Germans and were in consequence German citizens. These we were determined to get out of Germany. In raising the subject I emphasized that I quite understood the German point of view that it was the duty of all German citizens to take their share of the burden imposed by the existing situation, but I pointed out how desirable it was that these women who had lost their homes, or whose husbands and grown-up sons were either killed or missing, should be removed to Sweden, where they could be looked after by their relatives. The Swedish Legation had prepared lists of these people, and I now handed Himmler several containing only the most distressing cases. His face clouded over when he discovered that the list included a number of children.

"I don't feel inclined to send German children to Sweden," he said. "There they will be brought up to hate their country, and they will be spat at by their playmates because their fathers were German." When I tried to calm him down by pointing out that it should be a comforting thought to German fathers to know that their children were in safety in Sweden, he retorted: "Their fathers would doubtless much rather see them grow up in a shack in Germany than have them given refuge in a castle in a country as hostile to Germany as Sweden is."

Nevertheless he gave the lists to Schellenberg, who later told me that I might look upon the matter as settled. He said he would himself see to it that there was no hitch.

Our conversation now became more general, and the head of the Gestapo led it around to the bolshevik menace. His argument followed much the same pattern as Ribbentrop's. He predicted the end of Europe if the German eastern front were to break down, for the second World War was a war between Europeans and Asiatics. There would be no future for Europe if the Allies were victorious. In just the last weeks more than a hundred thousand German women of ages from sixteen to eighty had been violated by the Russian hordes. He simply could not understand Sweden's blindness in the face of the immense danger from the East.

Bernadotte: "But Germany was allied to Russia during part of this war. How does that fit in with what you have just said?"

Himmler: "I thought you would say that. We made a mistake, but we soon realized that the Russian armed might was so great that it was only a question of time when it would be turned against us."

In the course of this visit to Germany I obtained fairly reliable evidence that Himmler had been opposed throughout the war to an attack on Sweden. His opponent in this had always been Ribbentrop, who had favored such a course.

Even while we sat there talking about past events and conditions, the fighting front for which he was responsible—it was at no great distance from us—was beginning to crack, just as Germany was beginning to crack, and everyone knew that the end was not far off.

Himmler returned to the subject of Sweden, saying: "It is with the deepest gratitude and admiration that we Germans recall Sweden's humanitarian acts during the first World War. During this war we have not seen much evidence of that sort, but we nevertheless have a certain regard for Sweden. As an evidence of it I can mention the fact that we did not bother to occupy you in 1941. It would have been a simple matter then."

Bernadotte: "That may be true, but it would not be quite so simple now."

Himmler: "As a matter of fact, we never even thought of occupying either Sweden or Switzerland, in spite of what your press alleges. Speaking of your press, I can tell you I had decided that no Norwegian students were to be sent to Germany, but when I learned of the menacing tone of the Swedish papers and their threats I at once gave orders for the removal of the students to Germany."

Bernadotte: "The Swedish press showed itself critical of the Allies, too—for instance, after the Crimean conference, and again when certain persons were placed on the black list."

Himmler: "I can't say I have noticed that. As for the black list, I suppose I head it."

I explained that the black list was not a roster of war criminals, but concerned commercial matters. Himmler laughed and said that in that case it did not concern him.

At the beginning of this century a boy was

growing up in South Germany whose name was to become known throughout the world. He came of a simple middle-class family, and his father had been tutor to one of the princes of the Bavarian royal house. During the Great War the boy enlisted in the Bavarian Guards and attained the rank of sergeant major at the age of sixteen. When the war ended he returned home and joined the Nazi movement at its very inception.

"Those were glorious days," said Himmler. (He had been talking of his own life.) "We members of the movement were in constant danger of our lives, but we were not afraid. Adolf Hitler led us and held us together. They were the most wonderful years of my life. Then I could fight for what I regarded as Germany's rebirth." He ended by saying that, after all, the movement had produced real benefits, particularly in respect to social legislation. He failed to make any mention of the millions of Jews who had been murdered while "the movement" was in power. During this conversation I was also struck by the incongruity of a supreme commander of the German home army in the last phase of World War II with no higher military training than that of a sergeant major under Wilhelm II.

While we were talking about various matters I asked him if he would not admit that there were decent people among the Jews, just as there were among all races. I told him that I had many Jewish friends. To my surprise he admitted that I was right, but added that we in Sweden had no Jewish problem and could therefore not understand the German point of view. An indication that Himmler had lately changed his attitude towards the Jews could probably be found in his agreement with Musy. Later on Himmler, at my suggestion, agreed that, if the necessity should arise, he would allow interned Jews to be handed over to the Allied military authorities instead of having them removed from the concentration camps where they were held.

Before leaving, I returned to the subject of the Scandinavian prisoners who were to be collected in two camps. Obviously, I said, our ideas as to the numbers involved were greatly at variance. I therefore asked for reassurance that the persons liberated should include civilians in the concentration camps. Himmler gave me this assurance and promised to let me have, before I returned to Sweden, definite answers to the questions we had discussed. When I said good-by to him he turned to Schellenberg and asked him if he had chosen a good chauffeur for me. Schellenberg replied that he had got the best man he could, the journey to Berlin being rather dangerous because of the many tank traps and barricades that had been put up on the roads. "Good," said Himmler. "Otherwise it might happen that the Swedish papers would announce in big headlines: 'WAR CRIMINAL HIMMLER MURDERS COUNT BERNADOTTE.' " With these words he left the room.

Herr von Ribbentrop was affable and helpful. When on Wednesday, February 21st I called on him at the Foreign Office to tell him, as agreed, of the outcome of my talk with Himmler, he raised no difficulties. A memorandum had already informed him of the subjects I had discussed with Himmler, and he told me that he would not oppose the assembling of the Norwegian and Danish prisoners in two camps, and that Swedish-born women would be given exit visas for Sweden. He pointed out, however, that the German authorities could not undertake to arrange transportation, as all vehicles were required for the war. The Swedish Red Cross must provide its own transport, as well as fuel. Herr von Ribbentrop seemed pleased when I told him that this could easily be arranged, and that I would accompany the column. He promised to support me with Himmler and to assist me in every way. Then he returned to his favorite subject. Referring to the latest developments in the situation, principally the bombing of Dresden and Nürnberg and the consequences, he asserted that there was a growing inclination among the Nazis towards Communism. I then said good-by to Herr von Ribbentrop and left him.

Himmler kept his word and let me have a definite decision before I started for home. Immediately after my visit to Ribbentrop I lunched with Brigadeführer Schellenberg. He told me that Himmler had several times talked to him about my visit, which had pleased him. Schellenberg was authorized to inform me that Himmler had definitely given his consent to the proposals I had submitted to him: Swedish-born women were to receive exit visas (with the reservation that, if any of them had had any trouble with the police, such cases should be submitted to him personally for examination), and the Norwegian and Danish prisoners were to be assembled in a camp at Neuengamme, not far from Hamburg. I was further given permission to establish contact with Professor Seip (as a matter of fact, I had already done so), who had been liberated and now represented Norwegian interests in Germany, as well as with the Danish Legation in Berlin. For my part I promised to endeavor to have my Red Cross column ready at Warnemünde ten days later.

STOCKHOLM–BERLIN–FRIEDRICHSRUH–STOCKHOLM

March 1945

It was with an easier mind that I returned to Stockholm. The foundations had been laid. It should be possible to save many lives, and Sweden could be of real help to her Scandinavian neighbors. On my return I immediately reported to the Swedish Government. It approved my arrangements with Himmler and von Ribbentrop and also agreed to my suggestion that a Red Cross detachment be dispatched at government expense, the equipment and material to be supplied by the military authorities. I also reported to the commander-in-chief, General Helge Jung, who gave the plan his approval. The work of organizing the expedition was immediately begun by the Defense Staff and the Army General Staff. As the

Count Folke Bernadotte rejoins his wife and their son on his return from one of his trips to Germany

Reichsführer SS Heinrich Himmler

German authorities had stipulated that the number of personnel must not exceed two hundred and fifty, the detachment was composed as follows: three platoons, each of twelve busses, and one platoon of twelve trucks. The detachment further included mobile field kitchens, workshops, ambulances, and a quartermaster's platoon. Colonel Gottfrid Björck was appointed leader of the expedition. All the personnel were volunteers chosen from regulars and conscripts in the armed forces. The military insignia on their uniforms were replaced by those of the Red Cross. After the detachment had been assembled in Skåne, the southernmost Swedish province, it was dispatched by boat to Denmark via Malmö. On March 11th it was in Odense, where the Danish Red Cross had arranged billeting and meals. The municipality and townspeople showed us magnificent hospitality, and everything was done by the Danish authorities to facilitate our journey.

On March 12th we crossed the Danish-German frontier. Our route was planned to go via Flensburg, Kiel, and Lübeck to Schloss Friedrichsruh, which was to be our headquarters. We reached our destination late at night on the same day and were welcomed by the owners of the castle, Prince Otto von Bismarck and his wife, a daughter of the Swedish architect Ivar Tengbom. During our whole stay they helped our work with all manner of practical arrangements, besides showing us great hospitality and kindness.

A telephone message from Berlin: Obergruppenführer Kaltenbrunner was on the warpath, and others in Himmler's immediate entourage as well. This information came from the most reliable source: Brigadeführer Schellenberg, who had very intimate contact with the Swedish Legation in Berlin. Kaltenbrunner was trying to wreck my arrangement with Himmler. On several occasions he had said to the Danish representatives in Berlin that I must be very innocent if I imagined that Swedish Red Cross delegates would be permitted access to the German concentration camps, and that to allow Danish and Norwegian prisoners to be transported to Sweden was unthinkable. Kaltenbrunner's reasoning was not difficult to follow. Not only did the Swedish plan appear to him wholly unnecessary, but it was intolerable from the point of view of the Third Reich. If the program were sanctioned, neutral representatives would obtain far too intimate a view of conditions in the various camps, the long and carefully preserved secret of their horrors would be revealed, and the last remnants of Nazi prestige would vanish. When this telephone message came from the Swedish Legation, I replied emphatically that I would not permit my arrangements with Himmler to be interfered with by any subordinate, and that I declined to discuss these matters with anyone but Himmler personally. The decisions taken could only be revoked by a new agreement between Himmler and myself. I said this, not doubting that our telephone line was tapped and that the conversation would soon reach Kaltenbrunner's ears.

This episode gives an interesting side light on the conditions prevailing during the last grim act of the Nazi drama. The agony of death had begun; dissolution had already set in; but intrigue and counter-intrigue among the hierarchy were as vindictive as ever. I know that Schellenberg played an active and useful part in these days which were so critical for our mission; in fact, I do not believe that it would have been brought to a successful conclusion but for his powerful support. He told me later that Himmler had said that the promise he had given me must not be broken. Himmler himself later gave me an account of what he had experienced during this interval; he had had to overcome very strong opposition to get the scheme carried through. He added, sadly, that the order and efficiency formerly displayed by his subordinates had gravely deteriorated as a result of Germany's precarious military situation. And meanwhile the Allied fronts were getting closer and closer to Germany's heart.

It became clear to me that I must return to Berlin. On March 5th I flew to Berlin, where I at once began negotiations with Schellenberg as well as with his antagonist Kaltenbrunner. The latter now came into the open as my opponent.

Kaltenbrunner: "I do not intend to assist you in this matter you have brought up."

Bernadotte: "And I am not going to stand one of Himmler's subordinates trying to sabotage an arrangement agreed upon between him and myself."

The gloves were off. The fight had begun.

Half a century earlier the political world had its eyes sharply focused on Schloss Friedrichsruh, for it was to Friedrichsruh that the aged Chancellor Otto von Bismarck had withdrawn after his forced resignation in March 1890. It was from here that he carried on his campaign against the "new course" of German policy. It was here that he wrote his highly critical articles about William II and also his famous *Gedanken und Erinnerungen.* It was at Friedrichsruh that he received the homage of the German people; here vast numbers came as on a pilgrimage to manifest their love for the aged statesman. And it was here that he ended his days.

Now Friedrichsruh had become the headquarters of a Swedish errand of mercy in the final stages of the second World War. The old Castle was shortly to find itself in the thick of the fighting.

On March 9th I went to Friedrichsruh to await

the arrival of the Red Cross detachment. Our work during March included transporting three large contingents to Neuenburg—specifically, 2200 Danes and Norwegians from the concentration camp at Sachsenhausen, to the north of Berlin; 600 Scandinavians from Dachau, near Munich; and 1600 policemen from various camps northwest of Dresden. The transferrals from Sachsenhausen were carried out in seven relays between March 15th and March 30th. As soon as we had made sure of a supply of gasoline a column of thirty-five vehicles was formed for the run to Dachau, a round-trip distance of eleven hundred miles. The column left on March 19th, under the command of Colonel Björck personally, and by March 24th the task had been completed without any mishaps. Finally, at the end of March, the Danish policemen had been collected from the various camps.

It is not necessary for me to enter into a detailed account of the work of the expedition, as I understand that this will be the subject of a special report.

Another of the Bismarck estates was to play a

part in the events of those days: Schönhausen, one hundred and twenty-five miles east of Berlin. It was on this family estate that the Iron Chancellor was born and brought up, and there, no doubt, he absorbed the Junker ideals to which he remained faithful throughout his life. Now the Swedish Legation had been installed at Schönhausen, and during my work in Berlin we motored to the capital from the old manor almost every morning. These drives gave one a pretty clear picture of conditions in Germany two months before capitulation. All main roads were barricaded, and one could see men of the Volkssturm as well as prisoners of war working on the barricades. All cars and, for that matter, all travelers on the roads were subjected to the most careful control. I had, however, been provided by the Ministry of Police with a pass that enabled me to proceed unhindered.

On my first drive from Schönhausen to Berlin I saw for the first time women prisoners from concentration camps. There were hundreds of them—foreign women as well as Germans suspected of having worked against the Nazi regime

—guarded by male and female warders as they marched wearily to their work. It was a dreadful sight. A painful sight, too, were the long lines of German refugees from East Prussia. By the time we passed them it must have been weeks since these people had abandoned their homes. They were being directed to different centers where the local authorities would be responsible for billeting and feeding them. They appeared worn and weary and utterly hopeless. There was no future for them, and the present was a living hell. Whatever they had possessed was lost, material goods as well as any belief in the future. Silently the pitiable procession moved on, along roads lined with the carcasses of emaciated horses that had drawn the primitive vehicles used by the refugees until their strength gave out. These vehicles were reminiscent of the covered wagons used by the early settlers of the West in America. The tarpaulin or similar covering with which they had been hastily fitted was the only protection available for the women and children at night, and I was told that earlier in the year thousands of refugees had frozen to death. The winter had been very severe in Silesia and East Prussia.

Travel in those days was chaotic. The only way was by car, for trains took an incredible time. But motoring was not free from excitement, for German fighter planes and German anti-aircraft fire had almost ceased to exist during the last months of the war, and Allied airmen were able to attack all vehicles on the roads without interference. My car was painted white and bore the Red Cross flag as well as a Swedish flag, but this was not of much help. The Allied authorities had announced in Stockholm that, because of the intensification of the air war, immunity for the Swedish Red Cross vehicles could not be guaranteed.

I recollect one day at the end of March when I was on my way from Schönhausen to Friedrichsruh. We had just passed the small town of Perleberg, halfway between Berlin and Hamburg, when we heard the sound of explosions. It was an Allied air raid on Perleberg. Presently, as we drove on, we saw six American bombers approaching us at low altitude. My chauffeur and I jumped out of the car and took cover behind some trees. A moment later the bombers swept over us at a height of only about thirty feet. I readily admit that I felt cold shivers down my spine, but our luck held. The Americans attacked an objective a few hundred yards from where we were and then disappeared.

But my most exciting drive came a little later. On April 20th I left Friedrichsruh to go to Berlin, where I had a meeting with Himmler. The war in the air had by then become so intensified that I was advised to take special precautions. I took two chauffeurs, one of whom, seated on the traveling trunk at the back of the car, was to act as observer. He was instructed to signal by banging the top of the car as soon as he saw Allied planes approaching, thus warning us to stop, jump out, and take whatever cover we could find. On our way we passed through the town of Nauen, twenty-six miles west of the capital. We noticed blue and yellow flags, a signal that an air raid was on, but as nothing seemed to be happening we continued on our way until we reached the outskirts of the town. Seeing an old woman by the side of the road, we pulled up, and I asked her if a raid was on. Before she had time to reply, we heard the dull drone of a large number of Allied bombers. A few seconds later bombs were dropped on the railway station, less than a hundred yards away. We drove on out of the town and took cover in a trench that had been dug at the side of the road for the defense of the adjoining village, the plan apparently being to sweep the road with fire from anti-tank guns.

There was brilliant sunshine and a cloudless sky as the Allied bombers swooped on towards their targets. For about an hour we lay in our trench, gazing at the fascinating spectacle of Nauen and neighboring villages under heavy attack. We could see the bombs leaving the planes, after which what looked like a white column of smoke rushed towards the ground at great speed, and then there came a terrifying explosion. This was the first time I had observed anything approaching panic among the German population. A crowded shelter had been hit, a number of people killed, and men and women came running across the fields, aimlessly seeking shelter in ditches and anything that offered cover of any kind. It was as if the people of Nauen felt that nothing could save them, since not even a few fighters from the near-by airfield of Spandau went up to engage the enemy.

A few days later in Denmark I had another proof of the paralysis that had seized the Luftwaffe. A Danish ambulance plane had been put at my disposal, and we were just about to take off from a German airfield at Skustrup, in southern Jutland, when the air raid warning was sounded and we saw American fighters attacking some military installations near by. As we got hastily out of our plane, the American fighters were coming towards us at great speed. We threw ourselves into a trench, and almost at the same instant nine fighters roared over our heads, machine guns going full blast. The attack lasted for several hours. When it was over I sought out the German commandant and asked him why he had not ordered some of his own machines to go up, for I had seen them, well camouflaged, on the outlying parts of the airfield. He shrugged his shoulders and replied: "Oh, I have the machines all right, but not a drop of gasoline, so they are of no use to me at all."

German troops were retreating over the roads near Hamburg, at Neu-Brandenburg, and near other towns—small disorganized groups, almost without arms, almost as hopeless as the refugees from the east; soldiers who realized that the war was lost, that this was the end. I noticed groups of almost platoon strength, unarmed but for a couple of rifles. When I remarked on this to German officers they replied resignedly that such was unfortunately the fact. Supply of arms had ceased. The few weapons that remained had to be husbanded. When men were relieved they had to pass their weapons along to those who took over. And this was the army that a few years before, in 1940–1, so nearly conquered all Europe.

As soon as I had seen the work of the Swedish Red Cross detachment well under way I set out for Denmark to report to the Danish authorities on our negotiations and the work that we had set in motion. Just before my arrival in Copenhagen the Shell building had been bombed. It was the headquarters of the Gestapo in Denmark, and since they naturally expected an attack sooner or later, they resorted to a typical measure to prevent its being carried out: they placed a number of Danish Fighters for Freedom in cells on the top floor. The Allies had decided, however, that the building must nevertheless be bombed. When I arrived there was great excitement and jubilation over the highly successful bombing raid. The majority of the imprisoned Fighters for Freedom had miraculously escaped death, while the voluminous archives of the Gestapo had been destroyed by fire. Unhappily, a number of children in a school near the Shell building had lost their lives.

My audience with King Christian deeply affected me. I had learned enough to realize that he was as important today to the Freedom movement as he had ever been. To the Danish people he was the focal point of their resistance, the supreme head of the Freedom movement. Now, sitting in his invalid chair—he had not yet recovered from injuries resulting from a fall from his horse some years before—he was moved to tears as he listened to my account. He expressed his great joy at the results we had so far achieved, and I assured him that we would not stop until we had reached the goal we had set ourselves—till all Danes and Norwegians in the concentration camps had been brought over to Sweden.

I returned to Sweden and arrived in Stockholm on March 22nd.

NEUENGAMME–HOHEN-LÜCHEN

March 28th–April 9th

Nearing the German coast by air, we received a radio report that a heavy daylight attack on Berlin was in progress, and we were able to make out a number of planes in the distance. As it was impossible to distinguish if they were Allied or German, our pilot decided to make a landing at Stralsund. Just as we were circling over the air-field another message reported all clear, and we resumed our flight and soon reached the German capital. It was a sea of flame. A pall of thick smoke covered all the surrounding country, and when Richert, our Minister, met me at the Tempelhof airfield, he told me the all-clear had sounded only half an hour before.

What had brought me back after only a few days' absence was my anxiety lest the activities of the Swedish Red Cross should suffer a setback. My own experience had told me how very unstable the situation was. Anything might happen, and if something did, I wanted at least to be on the spot.

And something did. In Berlin I was informed that our people had not yet been allowed to begin their work at Neuengamme. The German authorities had raised difficulties, insisting that the camp must be put in order before we could do anything. According to the agreement, part of Neuengamme was to be set aside for the Scandinavian prisoners, and there was evidently no desire to admit any foreigners until things had been tidied up. Norwegian prisoners informed me later that sanitary measures had been begun in the camps a few weeks before, and that conditions had improved considerably in the section where the Scandinavians were to be placed. I have, therefore, good reason to believe that the hideous conditions at a later date revealed in, for example, Buchenwald had existed in Neuengamme too.

It was on Good Friday, March 30th, that I was

given the first opportunity to visit the concentration camp, where several thousand Scandinavian prisoners had already been assembled by the Swedish Red Cross.

The Third Reich was now not merely crumbling: it was about to collapse. In the west the British and the Americans had already crossed the Rhine and were advancing on Osnabrück. In the east the Russians were pressing forward; they were to enter the suburbs of Vienna a few days later, simultaneously with the sensational Allied advance towards Bremen-Verden. On April 10th Königsberg and Vienna were taken by the Russians. The goal was Berlin.

We drove up to the entrance of Neuengamme, where the gates were opened for us and closed as soon as we were inside. I was the first representative of a neutral humanitarian organization to visit a concentration camp, for when our people had collected prisoners from the various camps they had not been allowed to enter; instead, the prisoners had been assembled outside the gates, where the motor coaches and ambulances were waiting. It was with feelings of great emotion that I prepared to see these, the most revolting creations of the Third Reich, which had aroused such feelings of horror and fear throughout the whole world. Neuengamme was not a bad test case, for it was believed to be one of the worst—quite on a par with the Dachau camp near Munich, notorious since the Nazis' first seizure of power.

The commandant, Obersturmbannführer Pauli, received us in his green SS uniform, looking very smart and military and efficient, an expert in his own field. He had been in Poland, and at Lublin he had given incontrovertible proof that he understood how to keep concentration-camp prisoners in order. As a matter of fact, he had the reputation of being one of the very worst representatives of his profession, if it can be called that. However, he showed me the utmost courtesy, was helpful and reasonable, and agreed to almost everything I suggested. The guns were roaring near Bremen, the front was approaching nearer and nearer to Berlin, and the Obersturmbannführer probably realized that his professional days were numbered.

While in America I had met Odd Nansen, the

brilliant young architect son of the famous explorer Fridtjof Nansen; we had worked together there until 1940 and become great friends. When he was brought before me and I saw him snatch off his cap and stand to attention as all prisoners were required to do when in the presence of a German of rank—the commandant was with me—I boiled with anger at this example of German so-called discipline. Odd Nansen was one of those Norwegians who had risked everything, one of the many sent to concentration camps. Here they were, then, all these Scandinavian patriots. We had been able to obtain a complete list, for in our previous negotiations with the Germans it had been agreed that every prisoner collected by the Swedish detachment should be given a form on which to enter his name and the state of his health. At first the Germans had objected, but I understand that we outmaneuvered them by pointing out that we should be responsible for getting the prisoners in our charge to Neuengamme, and that we could not accept this responsibility without a list of names. We were thus very quickly in possession of complete statistics concerning all the

Scandinavian prisoners at Neuengamme and able to transmit them forthwith to the Danish and Norwegian authorities and organizations concerned.

I well remember the first hutments I inspected. The commandant, who accompanied me everywhere, made no objections when I wanted to speak to the prisoners and even agreed to my speaking with them in Swedish, though I thought it wiser not to carry on long conversations in that language, in order not to make him suspicious. In this particular building were lodged the Danish policemen who had been deported to Germany when the German occupation authorities in Denmark suppressed the regular police. Some of these men had been at Neuengamme before, after which they had been moved to other camps. They had shown little enthusiasm when told they were going back to this camp, where their experiences had been the worst possible. And when I looked around I could well understand their feelings. The discipline was evidently barbarous and the overcrowding appalling. In most of the huts wooden pallets had been laid on the floor, and these, covered with sacks, made up the prisoners' beds. What it would be like if an epidemic were to break out could easily be imagined. Among the prisoners were Norwegians and Danish doctors who had done all they could to help their comrades. Assisted by them, we at once set about improving matters. The Swedish Red Cross had obtained permission to send a number of delegates to work inside the camps, and under the leadership of Professor Gerhard Rundberg they lost no time in beginning to improve the sanitary conditions. Odd Nansen, who had already drawn up a plan showing how the hospital barracks should be reconstructed, was wonderfully helpful. We also arranged for medicines and portable buildings to be sent to Neuengamme from Denmark.

One episode of this visit stands out especially in my memory. We had arranged to hold a conference in one of the hospital barracks. There were present, not only representatives of the camp authorities, but also, at my invitation, the Danish and Norwegian doctors, as well as delegates chosen by the prisoners. Something tremendous had entered into the existence of these men, for it was certainly the first time they had been invited to take part in a discussion, seated at a conference table. It was touching to see how their spirits rose, how their faces lit up, how hope was reborn, when I was able to tell them that in a few days they would be sent back to Denmark.

When I took my departure the Danes and Norwegians gathered along the enclosure of electrified wire that surrounded the camp. I called to them "Paa gjensyn" (Danish for "Au revoir"), saw the joy in their eyes, and trusted they really understood that we had no intention of going away before accomplishing the task we had set ourselves. But I thought, too, of the prisoners of whom I had caught a glimpse in a part of the camp where there were no Scandinavians, and where we had no power. There were thousands of unhappy human beings there, or rather human wrecks, wandering aimlessly about the camp, apathetic, vacant, incapable of ever returning to a normal existence.

The military situation was now developing at such a pace that Neuengamme would inevitably soon be in the fighting zone, and I had a serious talk with the commandant about the state of affairs. I told him that if it became necessary to evacuate the camp, he must see that the Danes and Norwegians were sent north, either to northern Schleswig or to Denmark. The great advantage gained by having them all assembled in one camp near the Danish frontier must not be lost. Obersturmbannführer Pauli promised to see that my wish was carried out; whereupon I started for Berlin and my second meeting with Himmler.

The meeting was on April 2nd. As before, I visited Himmler at the Sanatorium of Hohen-Lüchen, administered by Professor Gebhardt, whose friendship with Himmler went back to their school days. When the SS Chief entered the room I noticed that he was not only somber, but also nervous. During our talk, which went on for four hours, he did not attempt to deny that he regarded the situation as most critical, although he would not admit that it was hopeless. It was during this long conversation that my activities in Germany were to be given a new direction. I suddenly realized that I had been dragged into the vortex of high politics.

Himmler: "I am ready to do anything for the German nation, but the war must go on. I have given my oath to the Führer, and that oath is a binding one."

Bernadotte: "Don't you realize that Germany has lost the war? By attacking Russia in 1941 you yourselves made it a war on two fronts, and it was that which snatched victory from your grasp. You yourself say that you are willing to do anything for the German nation, and if that is true, and if you consider his determination to continue the war a disaster to your country, involving the death of tens of thousands more on the fighting fronts as well as on the domestic front, you ought to put the welfare of your people above your loyalty to Hitler. A person in your position, bearing such an enormous responsibility, cannot obey a superior blindly, but must have the courage to accept responsibility for decisions made in the interest of the people."

Himmler did not answer. A few moments later, called to the telephone, he rose quickly and left the room. Brigadeführer Schellenberg, who was again present at our talk, turned to me and asked if I could not see Eisenhower to discuss with him the possibilities of arranging a capitulation on the Western front. I told him that this was quite impossible, that the initiative must come from Himmler, and that I was unwilling to act as intermediary, since my doing so might be taken to indicate a belief that Eisenhower and the Western Allies would be willing to negotiate for an armistice. I said I was convinced that this was not the fact.

Himmler returned, and we began to discuss the transporting of Danes and Norwegians and the camp at Neuengamme. I told him that on the whole the transportations had been successful, but that conditions in the camp, which I had inspected, were vile. I repeated again, emphasizing the fact that at that time tens of thousands of German refugees were being sent to Denmark, that all Danish and Norwegian prisoners should be allowed removal to Sweden. Himmler answered that personally he would grant my request with pleasure, but that he could not possibly do so. The hand of Hitler was to be felt here. Hitler was opposed, and Himmler did not dare oppose him. At this point, however, Himmler began to compromise. "One possibility," he said, "would be to let *some* of the prisoners leave now. If all were to be sent at the same time, it would attract too much attention." I immediately put forward a program—it was immediately accepted—calling for the dispatch to Sweden of all the Swedish and Norwegian women and all the invalids, together with a small proportion of the 461 Norwegian students in Neuengamme. (The actual number was to be decided later.) All of the Danish policemen were to be sent to Denmark. The Scandinavians sent to Sweden were not to be interned, but placed in hospitals or boarded out. They would, however, be required to give an undertaking not to return to Norway or Denmark or to go to England, but to remain in Sweden till the war was over. Subject to the same condition, Himmler further agreed to the release of a certain number of interned Norwegian civilians, among them Professor Seip, and some French citizens.

I had made progress, and the situation looked more hopeful from my point of view, but Himmler was filled with gloom.

Himmler: "The German Government has made fatal mistakes. It was a mistake not to be more frank with England. As for me—well, of course, I am regarded as the cruelest and most sadistic man alive. But one thing I want to put on record: I have never publicly vilified Germany's enemies."

Bernadotte: "If you haven't, Hitler has done so all the more thoroughly. What was it he said?—'We shall wipe out every one of the English cities.' Is it, then, so surprising that the Allies systematically bomb German towns?" Himmler retorted that bombing was not started by the Germans, and I reminded him of Warsaw in 1939 and Rotterdam in 1940. To this he said nothing; and shortly afterwards he rose with the remark that he had to discuss some routine matters with Schellenberg. The audience was over.

Schellenberg accompanied me to Berlin, talking the whole way in a confidential but rather forced manner. What he related gave me a good picture of what was happening behind the German political scene. He told me that after my departure Himmler had continued the subject of capitulation in the West and, but for Hitler, would unhesitatingly have asked me to go to Eisenhower. However, he had hinted, the situation might change; Hitler's position might be shaken; at any moment— Himmler had asked Schellenberg to convey to me his hope that, in that event, I would proceed immediately to Allied headquarters. Continuing, Schellenberg said that Himmler was in a very difficult position, being torn between his desire to save Germany from utter chaos and his loyalty to the Führer. Finally he uttered a warning: Obergruppenführer Kaltenbrunner, chief of the Security Police and possessor of great influence over Hitler, was furious at the concessions Himmler had granted me, and Kaltenbrunner was a very dangerous man. Himmler had therefore told Schellenberg to caution me against telephoning about the matters we had discussed, for Kaltenbrunner had given orders that all the telephone lines I might use should be discreetly tapped.

During the following days I had several more talks with Schellenberg, who had had further conferences with Himmler. He thought that the latter, together with other leading figures in the Nazi hierarchy, would soon decamp to the south of Germany. I advised Schellenberg in that event to remain in northern Germany and to obtain from Himmler broad discretionary powers, especially in connection with the Scandinavian prisoners of war, in order that if such a situation arose they might be removed to Sweden. He promised to do his best to make such arrangements. Then he informed me that Himmler had once more recurred to the question of my going to Eisenhower. At this point I told Schellenberg in plain words what my attitude in the matter was, and that he must rid his mind of any illusions that the Allies would ever enter into negotiations with Himmler. Himmler could not conceivably head the government for more than a short period of transition, after which it would be taken over by the Allied occupation authorities. It was possible, however, I added, that in this way Himmler might prevent Germany being plunged into utter chaos.

I then proceeded to specify my stipulations. I said that I was prepared to go to Eisenhower's headquarters on the following conditions:

1. There must be an announcement by Himmler that Hitler—compelled by illness to give up his powers—had chosen him to be the leader of the German people.

2. Himmler must declare the National Socialist Party dissolved and remove all Party officials.

3. Himmler must order the activity of the so-called Werewolves to cease.

4. Before my departure I must have confirmation from Friedrichsruh that orders had been given for the dispatch to Sweden of all Danish and Norwegian prisoners.

The acceptance and fulfillment of these conditions meant a revolution in Germany. They meant that Himmler would depose Hitler, dissolve the National Socialist Party, and put an end to the Third Reich. Personally, I never imagined Himmler would accept them. But Schellenberg did not hesitate. He told me that he would try to induce his chief to accept them.

Schellenberg also gave me on this occasion the information that Hitler had issued orders that the concentration camps at Buchenwald, Bergen-Belsen, and probably Theresienstadt as well should be evacuated and the prisoners compelled to cover a distance of about one hundred and ninety miles *on foot.* Schellenberg said that he had protested strongly against this order, and that after a stormy discussion he had succeeded in inducing Hitler to countermand it. The commandants of the camps had been instructed not to evacuate them, but to surrender the prisoners to the Allied troops. Similar instructions would be given in connection with Neuengamme.

Corruption was rife in Germany. With a packet of cigarettes, half a liter of spirits, or a small quantity of coffee one could do pretty much anything. I had good evidence of what could be done when I got out of my car at Tempelhof. I was accompanied by Professor Seip and his wife, who had joined her husband in captivity. Himmler had given his consent to their leaving the country, but their papers had not come through

Obergruppenführer Ernst Kaltenbrunner

Brigadeführer Walter Schellenberg

in time, and the authorities had informed us that they might go regardless. We had some moments of suspense at Tempelhof airfield, waiting to see how the local officials would act. A packet of cigarettes did the trick, and Professor Seip and his wife were allowed to go aboard the plane. After a short interval we took off. It seems to me that in all my travels in Germany I had never experienced such true happiness as I felt at that moment.

That was April 9th—five years to a day from the German invasion of Norway.

FRIEDRICHSRUH–BERLIN–HOHEN-LÜCHEN–FLENSBURG –LÜBECK

April 19th–24th

Ten days later General Patton had penetrated into Czechoslovakia. Northern Holland was liberated, resistance in Hamburg had been crushed, and the line defending Berlin was cracking under the Russian assault. Hitler issued the order: "Shoot any officers who order retreat."

When I climbed into the night train from Stockholm to Malmö on April 18th I knew that great events were imminent, but I had no idea how sensational they would be. On my arrival in Copenhagen on the morning of the 19th, I was flown to an airfield in South Jutland and was met by a delegate of the Swedish Red Cross at the Danish-German frontier. What he reported to me was very alarming. It appeared that a couple of days earlier the Danish Consul General in Hamburg had been in contact with Reichsstadthalter Karl Kauffmann, with whom he had arranged for the Scandinavian prisoners assembled at Neuengamme to be sent to Denmark immediately. When the Nazi party representative in Hamburg heard about this, he at once got in touch with Himmler, who evidently knew nothing about the arrangement. Himmler gave orders that no transportations of any kind should take place. He also stopped the transfer of sick Scandinavians that had been going on for some time between Neuengamme and Sweden.

The atmosphere at Friedrichsruh was gloomy when I arrived there, and it did not cheer me up when the German liaison officer informed me that in his opinion the chance of getting the transfers continued was very small. However, the same evening he looked me up after dinner and told me that the whole camp at Neuengamme was to be evacuated immediately and the prisoners transported to Denmark.

I subsequently heard the explanation of this sudden change of plan from Himmler himself.

The reason for the evacuation of the entire camp of Neuengamme was the publicity that the Allies had given to the conditions in the concentration camps at Buchenwald and Bergen-Belsen—though Himmler insisted that this publicity was a tissue of lies. I replied that in my opinion the persons who had reported these conditions were so trustworthy that one could not doubt the truth of their accounts. Himmler went completely off the deep end and gave me the following version of what had occurred: One of the Allies' tanks, it seems, for some reason burst into flames as it approached one of the camps, and the Allied officers, thinking this the result of firing by the German guards, opened fire on the camp, with the result that one of the buildings was set on fire. This, said Himmler, was the explanation of the many charred bodies found when the Allies entered the camp. "It is outrageous," the head of the Gestapo added, "that this camp, which in my opinion was in model shape, should have become the subject of these shameless accounts. Nothing has upset me so much as what the Allied press has published about this business."

The next day we started removing all the Scandinavians from Neuengamme. The success with which this task was carried out was due not least to the extraordinary assistance we received from the Danish Jutland corps, which, organized with the most commendable speed, arrived at Neuengamme only twelve hours later. The Scandinavians were saved; but what became of all the other prisoners, who numbered about 20,000? I don't know, and I was not present when the evacuation was carried out, but my Swedish comrades told me that it was hurried and brutal. The non-Scandinavians were pushed into freight trains whose destination no one knew. Questioned about it, the German commandant shrugged his shoulders: "Keine Ahnung" ("I have no idea"). The freight trains, like others of those ghostly trains that had so often steamed eastward in German-occupied countries in the years just past, disappeared in the distance with its human cargo and has not been heard of since.

April 20th–Adolf Hitler's birthday. Doctor Goebbels announced: "Our Führer has not deserted us. That is our victory." Two days later the Russian troops began to penetrate into Berlin.

It gave me a strange feeling to arrive in Berlin on this day that in other years had been celebrated with such enthusiasm by the Führer's faithful, devoted, idolatrous people. Now Berlin had become a silent city. The barricades were completed, and people wandered about waiting for what was going to happen.

An air-raid warning compelled me to spend several hours in the shelter of the Swedish Legation, after which I immediately sought out Brigadeführer Schellenberg. He informed me that Himmler was not to be found in Berlin. I pointed out that it was imperative for me to return to Friedrichsruh the following morning and asked him to do his utmost to arrange a meeting for sometime during the night of April 20th–21st. A few hours passed. Then came a message from Schellenberg asking me to proceed to Hohen-Lüchen Sanatorium, where I would be able to see Himmler in the course of the night. When I left Berlin in the afternoon I could hear the thunder of the Russian guns.

The roads were crowded with troops and refugees, and progress was not easy. However, we got to our destination by nine o'clock the same evening, and I was informed by Professor Gebhardt that he had not yet heard from Himmler. There was nothing to do but to wait. We dined, and I was shown over the hospital. It was filled with wounded soldiers from the Eastern front; I was even invited to be present when some of them were operated on. At half-past twelve there was a telephone message that Himmler would arrive at Hohen-Lüchen for breakfast at six in the morning.

The head of the Gestapo was a very spent and weary man when he entered the breakfast room at the appointed hour. Perhaps he felt he owed me some explanation, for he told me that he had slept hardly a wink for several nights. He gave the impression of being unable to remain long in one spot and of darting from place to place by way of outlet for his anxiety and restlessness.

The breakfast was both ample and excellent, and Himmler ate with a good appetite. Occasionally he tapped his front teeth with his fingernails—according to Schellenberg, a sure sign that he was in a state of nerves. This time our talk was entirely about humanitarian measures. I again put forward the request that the Scandinavian prisoners, who at the time were being transported to Denmark, should be allowed to continue the journey to Sweden; but Himmler once more refused. Schellenberg subsequently told me that Hitler had again forbidden any concession on this point.

Himmler, however, assented to some of my other requests. He agreed that, if Denmark should become a battleground, the Scandinavian prisoners of war were to be transported to Sweden under the auspices of the Swedish Red Cross. He also showed genuine interest in my proposal that the Swedish Red Cross be allowed to remove all French women interned at the Ravensbrück concentration camp. He said that he not only assented to this, but that he also wished us to remove the women of all nationalities, as the camp in question was shortly to be evacuated. I promised him that I would immediately give our detachment orders to this effect.

"The military situation is grave, very grave," Himmler remarked; but he showed no inclination to continue the subject.

I departed for Friedrichsruh immediately after breakfast. After a short visit to our headquarters, where I made arrangements for the removal of the women interned at Ravensbrück, I started for Denmark—to be precise, for the small town of Padborg, just north of the Danish-German frontier. There I had the opportunity of inspecting the excellent arrangements made by the Danish Red Cross and the Danish authorities for the reception and quartering of prisoners before they were removed to other places in Denmark. Here, too, I saw for the first time the well-known Fröslev camp, situated near Padborg. Because of the transportations from Germany that we had carried out during the past few days, the camp was very crowded, but spirits were high among the Danish and Norwegian prisoners. It is true that they were still being guarded by the Gestapo, that they were still under German orders, but the mere fact of having left Germany behind them made their hearts lighter. And certainly the Danish food was very different from what they had been given in Germany.

"Du gamla, du fria . . ." There they stood, these men and women who had risked their lives for their country, softly humming the Swedish national anthem, or whistling it under their breath. It was when I stepped out on to the steps of the hospital hut that I came upon this scene, perhaps the most moving of all. It was a salute that went straight to my heart. These people were still captives, but they felt freedom within reach. But they well knew what would happen if at that moment German camp discipline were to be enforced. In their desire to show their gratitude they risked that, and they could not have done it in a more beautiful manner.

At three o'clock the following morning I was awakened by a telephone call from the Gestapo chief at Flensburg, who informed me that Brigadeführer Schellenberg wished to speak to me about a most urgent matter. As I had promised to visit another Jutland camp prepared for Scandinavian prisoners of war arriving from Germany,

I was not able to go to Flensburg until later in the day. I met Schellenberg there at three in the afternoon.

That was on April 23rd. Schellenberg lost no time in letting off his bombshell. Hitler was finished. It was thought that he could not live more than a couple of days at the outside.

That same day Doctor Goebbels had announced that the Führer had arrived in Berlin, where he would personally lead the defence.

Schellenberg continued his report of the situation.

Schellenberg: "Himmler has decided to bring about a meeting with General Eisenhower to inform him that he is willing to give orders to the German forces in the West to capitulate. Would you be prepared to take this message to General Eisenhower?"

Bernadotte: "It would be better if Himmler's wishes were transmitted to the Swedish Government, who could then, if they were willing, transmit them to the representatives of the Western powers. But in no circumstances will I forward such a communiqué to the Swedish Minister for

Foreign Affairs, Mr. Günther, unless Himmler promises that the German forces in Norway and Denmark shall capitulate too. In any case it is most doubtful if the Western Allies will agree to capitulation on the Western front alone. But even if they should agree to it, there is no necessity for a personal meeting between Himmler and Eisenhower. Himmler need only give the order to the German supreme commander to lay down arms. And, as I have pointed out before, there is no question of Himmler's playing any part in the Germany of the future. At most, the Allies might want to use his services to carry out the surrender."

Schellenberg declared that he quite understood my points of view and would endeavor to make them clear to Himmler before the latter and I met again. We got through to Himmler on the telephone, and it was arranged that we should meet in Lübeck that night, the night of April 23rd–24th.

I shall not easily forget that night, with its uncanny feeling of disaster. Himmler arrived at the local branch of the Swedish Legation about half an hour before midnight. Immediately afterward the sirens began, and I asked Himmler if he wished to go down into the shelter. I could not promise, I added, that we should be left undisturbed, for naturally one could not prevent other occupants of the building or passers-by from taking cover. He hesitated a moment, then decided to go down. A small group of Swedes and Germans had already collected in the shelter, and Himmler talked to the Germans, evidently trying to find out what the popular feeling was. Obviously he was not recognized. During the hour that we spent in the shelter I looked curiously at him from time to time. He struck me as being utterly exhausted and at a nervous extremity; he looked as if he were mustering all his will power to preserve outward calm.

When the sirens shrieked "All clear" we left the shelter, sat down in one of the rooms of the Legation, and proceeded to discuss the subjects about which Himmler had come to consult me. It was now about half an hour after midnight.

There was no electric current, and two candles on our "conference table" provided the only illumination.

The head of the Gestapo began his review of the situation by saying that quite possibly Hitler was already dead, and that, if he were not, he certainly would be within the next few days. The Führer had gone to Berlin to die with the inhabitants of the capital. Berlin was surrounded, and it was only a question of a few days before it would fall. On the three previous occasions when we had met I had suggested to him, Himmler continued, that he should end the war. He said he had recognized that I was right—that the situation was hopeless, that the war must end and Germany admit herself defeated—but he had not been able to break his oath to the Führer. Now matters were different. It was quite possible that Hitler was already dead.

"I admit that Germany is defeated." The head of the Gestapo pronounced these words with a gesture of resignation. What was going to happen? Himmler, pursuing this line of thought, broached a subject of decisive importance to Europe; in fact, to the future of the whole world. In his own manner he touched on the importance of creating a Hitler legend—something that might very soon be launched, and that would play the same part after the fall of the Third Reich that the "stab in the back" played after the Peace of Versailles. Everything would depend, Himmler said, on how the Allies treated Germany. If the Allied nations meant to crush the German people, then Hitler would come to be regarded as the greatest of their heroes. It would be said that not only had Adolf Hitler been able to solve their internal problems: he had also raised them out of the "state of degradation" in which they had found themselves after the Peace of Versailles, in order finally to die the death of a hero at the head of his people, on the barricades of Berlin.

If I may be permitted to digress for a moment, I must say here that everything I have experienced and learned has firmly convinced me that the myth of Hitler's death while fighting on the barricades of his capital must be destroyed once for all, and as soon as possible. Adolf Hitler in the spring of 1945 was a mentally and physically sick man. A heroic act was the last thing of which he was capable. His decision to stay in Berlin was almost certainly due to his knowledge that, whatever happened, his days were numbered. For the German people, especially, it is of peculiar importance that this fact be made quite clear: There is nothing heroic in the manner of Adolf Hitler's death. The accounts of his last heroic fight are a pure myth. He died as a hunted man and as a cowardly man—as cowardly as all his henchmen showed themselves to be in the days of the breakup. The deadliest of all possibilities is that the German people will feel itself impelled to erect Adolf Hitler into a demigod on a pedestal.

The conference went on.

Himmler: "In the situation that has now arisen I consider my hands free. In order to save as great a part of Germany as possible from a Russian invasion I am willing to capitulate on the Western front in order to enable the Western Allies to advance rapidly towards the east. But I am not prepared to capitulate on the Eastern front. I have always been, and I shall always remain, a sworn enemy of bolshevism. In the beginning of the World War I fought tooth and nail against the Russo-German pact. Are you willing to forward a communiqué on these lines to the Swedish Minister for Foreign Affairs, so that he can inform the Western powers of my proposal?"

Bernadotte: "It is in my opinion quite impossible to carry out a surrender on the Western front and to continue fighting on the Eastern front. It can be looked upon as quite certain that England and America will not make any separate settlements with Germany."

Himmler: "I am well aware how extremely difficult this is, but all the same I want to make the attempt to save millions of Germans from a Russian occupation."

Bernadotte: "I am not willing to forward your communiqué to the Swedish Minister for Foreign Affairs unless you promise that Denmark and Norway shall be included in the surrender." Himmler replied without hesitation that he agreed to this, that he had no objections to American, British, or Swedish occupation of Denmark and

Norway, and that when that occurred the German troops would lay down their arms. He made only one reservation: neither Denmark nor Norway should be occupied by Russian troops. I asked Himmler what he proposed to do if he received a negative reply to his offer. He replied: "In that event I shall take over the command on the Eastern front and be killed in battle." As is known, he did not carry out his intention.

After pointing out again that I was extremely doubtful of the Western powers' acceptance of his proposal, I asked him to write a short letter to the Swedish Minister for Foreign Affairs, Günther, which I would hand to him as tangible evidence that Himmler really desired to make the necessary contact through me. Himmler immediately did as requested. He also declared that, if a meeting could be arranged between himself and Eisenhower, he was willing to make roughly the following declaration: "I recognize that German arms have suffered defeat at the hands of the Western powers. I am prepared to surrender unconditionally on the Western front, and also to discuss the technical ways and means of arranging capitulation of the German armed forces in Denmark and Norway."

This day was, Himmler declared, the bitterest of his life.

It was agreed that I should return to Sweden as quickly as possible and, through Schellenberg, let Himmler know the result of his move. Before going, I touched on two further questions. I told him that the executions in Denmark must cease; he must himself realize that they could only add fuel to the already burning hatred that the Danes felt towards Germany and the Germans. And I referred once more to the question of freeing King Leopold of Belgium. In both instances Himmler promised to grant my wish.

We departed from the Legation. It was about half-past three in the morning. Himmler insisted on driving the car himself, for he was now returning to the Eastern front. As luck would have it, he had no sooner started than he ran into the barbed wire that surrounded the building, and we had a terrific job to get the car clear. Our Secretary of Legation, Torsten Brandel, and our attaché, Count Axel Lewenhaupt, who witnessed our departure, agreed with me that there was something symbolical about the manner of Himmler's exit.

Later in the morning I returned with Schellenberg to Flensburg. He told me that Himmler had again spoken about his projected meeting with Eisenhower. He had tried to imagine the atmosphere of such a meeting, and had asked if Schellenberg thought he ought to make a bow to the Allied Supreme Commander and if he ought to shake hands.

Later in the morning of the same day I departed by ambulance plane for Copenhagen, and from there continued to Stockholm. At the Copenhagen airfield at Kastrup I was met by the Swedish Minister, Gustaf von Dardel. To him I reported all that had occurred; for communications between Stockholm and Schellenberg ought to go via the Swedish Minister in Copenhagen to our attaché, Lewenhaupt, whom I had asked to remain at Aabenraa.

STOCKHOLM–ODENSE–AABENRAA–COPENHAGEN–STOCKHOLM

April 24th–May 7th

On my arrival in Stockholm on April 24th I immediately called at the Foreign Office, where I met the Foreign Minister, Christian E. Günther, Erik C. Boheman, Permanent Under Secretary of State, and Eric von Post, head of the Political Department of the Foreign Office. This was at nine o'clock. An hour later Mr. Günther and I called on the Prime Minister, and at eleven o'clock we arrived at the Foreign Office, where I made my report. Himmler's proposal was directed exclusively to the Western Allies, a method of negotiation which, according to the officials of the Foreign Office, was not practicable in view of the obvious necessity of informing the Soviet Union. However, in order to inform the Allies of

Himmler's willingness to negotiate, which was in itself somewhat sensational, a meeting was held late that evening, at which were present the British Minister, Sir Victor Mallet, the American Minister, Mr. Herschel Johnson, Mr. Boheman, and myself. The two foreign diplomats pointed out that it was most unlikely that their governments would agree to Himmler's proposal, and that they must necessarily confer with the Moscow government.

Two more days passed. During the evening of April 26th Mr. Boheman rang me up to inform me that the American reply, signed by President Truman, had arrived. I went at once to the American Legation, where I found the Minister and Boheman. The telegram read:

"A German offer of surrender will be accepted only if it be complete on all fronts, as regards Great Britain and the Soviet Union as well as the United States. This condition fulfilled, the German forces on all fronts must immediately surrender to the local Allied commanders. Should resistance continue anywhere, the Allied attacks will be vigorously pressed until victory is complete."[1]

Mr. Boheman and I, on leaving the American Legation, went on to the residence of the Foreign Minister, who pointed out that the answer from the United States was far from unexpected. It was decided that I should leave Stockholm at once, meet Schellenberg, and hand the answer to him. Mr. Günther said that, if I went personally to present the answer, a break in the means of negotiation would be averted. On April 27th I flew to Odense, where I met Brigadeführer Schellenberg and presented the Western powers' reply to Himmler's offer of capitulation. At first it seemed to make him very depressed. There was now, he said, scarcely any possibility of a solution. After we had discussed the matter for a while he seemed to become more hopeful. In spite of everything he thought there might be a way to bring about a capitulation in Norway and Denmark, thus preventing these two countries from becoming

[1] Not the original text, but a retranslation from the Swedish. TRANSLATOR

theaters of war, with consequent devastation. We arranged to meet the following day in Lübeck in order to continue the discussion with Himmler.

I put up at the house of a Danish official, Amtman Thomsen, in Aabenraa, and there Brigadeführer Schellenberg called on me the following morning. He informed me that it was impossible for Himmler to get to Lübeck: he had departed for a place north of Bremen and wanted a meeting there. Schellenberg and I agreed that there was no point in my proceeding into the actual battle zone, but that he should go alone to acquaint Himmler with the situation.

This was on April 28th. When, later in the afternoon, I sat listening to news from the so-called "Atlantic" radio station, I heard my own name mentioned. This was followed by the announcement that according to reports from London and New York I had opened negotiations with the head of the SS, Reichsminister Himmler, for a German capitulation. My first thought was that this leak had spoiled everything and that there was no further possibility of negotiations.

On this point I have since somewhat altered my views. As a matter of fact, the publicity that my negotiations received at this early stage was to be of crucial importance, for it resulted in the alteration of a very important decision. From all appearances it seems that Himmler had been chosen from the beginning to be the leader of the Reich in the event of Hitler's death. The publication of Himmler's offer to surrender, however, overturned this arrangement. Instead of Himmler, Grand Admiral Karl Dönitz was appointed leader. It is very doubtful if the Allies could ever have entered into negotiations with Himmler, because of his terrible reputation. It was far easier with Dönitz. In the first place, he belonged to the armed forces, and any move on his part would be accepted by the military quite differently from any by Himmler. Also negotiations with him would be less distasteful to the Allies than negotiations with the head of the Gestapo. Himmler appears later to have told Schellenberg that he was much disappointed at having been passed over. On the other hand, he said, he looked upon the situation as so grave that all personal considerations must be sacrificed. He was therefore prepared to collaborate loyally with Dönitz. It is also my belief that Himmler maintained to the last that it was absolutely necessary at least to allow the German forces in Norway and Denmark to capitulate. In this he was strongly supported not only by Schellenberg, but also by the new Minister for Foreign Affairs, Count Schwerin von Krosigk.

Brigadeführer Schellenberg returned from his expedition on April 29th. He had found Himmler, he told me, at a place somewhere north of Bremen, but the meeting had not been a pleasurable one to him. Himmler had got news of the publicity that England and America had given to our negotiations, and he was furious. At one moment he had threatened to arrest Schellenberg as being the one who, together with me, had inveigled him into beginning negotiations. The next moment he had proposed that both he and Schellenberg place themselves under Colonel General Ferdinand Schörner's orders and attack the enemy on the Eastern front at the head of a battalion. Schellenberg gradually succeeded in calming him down, and after a couple of hours' discussion Himmler declared himself prepared to allow the German troops in Norway to capitulate, and also to allow the Germans in Denmark to lay down their arms to the British.

I telephoned Stockholm at once and requested that a representative of the Foreign Office proceed immediately to Copenhagen to meet Schellenberg. Having done that, I departed for Copenhagen with Schellenberg by car, and we arrived there the same evening.

The next day, April 30th, when I took up my negotiations again, Copenhagen was in a state of enormous excitement. There were all kinds of rumors, and the announcement that Germany had capitulated was expected at any moment. My negotiations with Himmler were now general knowledge, and it was believed that I had come to Copenhagen to discuss technical points in connection with the capitulation with Dr. Werner Best, the accredited representative of the Third Reich in Denmark. Enormous crowds had assembled at Kongens Nytorv outside the Hotel d'Angleterre in anticipation of further news.

During a conference at my hotel I heard firing

outside in the square, and when I went to the window I saw thousands of people running in every direction. Hipo-men had appeared in their cars and were sweeping the square with tommy-guns. The fusillade was, however, not very serious, and I could not see any casualties. But the incident made me understand better than anything before how great must be the Danes' hatred of the German invaders and, still more, of such of their countrymen as had entered into the service of the occupying power and become traitors to their own country. These Hipo-men, in their dark blue uniforms, made a vile impression on me. They were young hooligans enjoying the power they still possessed, well knowing it would soon be taken from them. To me, a member of a neutral nation, this episode had great significance. It gave me an insight into the sufferings of the Danish people during the hard and trying years of the occupation.

I conferred with the representative of the Swedish Foreign Office, von Post, and Schellenberg likewise with Dr. Best. After that I gave the King of Denmark a brief résumé of the situation.

Then Schellenberg, von Post, and I met at the Swedish Legation at half-past eleven, and Schellenberg reported his visit to Himmler. The Swedish view was, however, that further elucidation was required, and Schellenberg decided to make another trip to Himmler's headquarters.

Dr. Best was present at the subsequent luncheon at the Legation. It is said—I have heard it said by many Danes—that he tried to conduct himself as humanely as possible during the occupation, and that he several times intervened when the Gestapo became too brutal in their methods. I avoided all questions of high politics; but I asked him if he would agree to the transfer to Sweden of a number of Englishmen and Americans who had been interned in Denmark since the beginning of the war. He at once assented, saying that he would like this concession to be regarded as a personal favor to me, for he considered that he and his government owed a debt of gratitude to me for what I had done in connection with the exchange of German and Allied prisoners of war.

May 1st came, and with it, in the evening, the message for which millions of people had been waiting and longing for years: Hitler was dead. Grand Admiral Dönitz announced in his radio speech: "German men and women, soldiers of the German army, our Führer, Adolf Hitler, has fallen. The German people are bowed in sorrow and reverence. . . . The Führer has appointed me to be his successor." And in an order of the day to the German army Dönitz declared: "The greatest hero in the history of Germany has departed from the scene."

To me this heroic death meant, so far as I could see, that the point of departure of my negotiations had been shifted. Earlier that day, immediately after my return to Stockholm, I had had a conference with Günther and Boheman, and I still believed then that a solution could be found for the problem of capitulation. Now all these hopes were shattered. It was no longer Himmler who occupied the dominant position, but Grand Admiral Dönitz, who had been chosen instead as Hitler's successor. And Dönitz urged the continuation of the struggle: "I take over the supreme command of all branches of the armed forces with the intention of carrying on the war. . . ."

The picture, however, changed rapidly. On the evening of May 4th von Post, who had returned to Stockholm on the previous evening, informed me that Schellenberg had returned to Copenhagen and there had reported some sensational events. In the first place Grand Admiral Dönitz had decided to surrender, with all German forces in Holland, northwestern Germany, and Denmark. Secondly, Schellenberg was to reach Stockholm the following morning with authority from Dönitz to arrive at an understanding regarding a German surrender in Norway. At ten o'clock on the morning of May 5th Schellenberg, who had been nominated envoy, arrived at Stockholm by special plane, and immediately a meeting took place at my residence, "Dragongården," between him, von Post, and myself. Schellenberg presented his credentials, signed by Dönitz, and stated that the new German Minister for Foreign Affairs, Count Schwerin von Krosigk, had asked him to try to arrange a meeting with General Eisenhower to discuss a general German surrender.

Schellenberg gave us some other interesting information. At Mürwick, in the neighborhood of

Flensburg, he had had a long meeting with Dönitz, Schwerin von Krosigk, and Himmler, at which were also present Field Marshal Keitel and Colonel General Alfred Jodl. On this occasion Schellenberg said that he had been able to persuade the government to order the capitulation of all German troops in Holland, northwestern Germany, and Denmark. The only one who had violently opposed this order was Keitel. Von Post told Schellenberg that the Swedish Government naturally felt it necessary to inform the representatives of the Allied powers in Stockholm of what had been going on. Schellenberg expressed the wish that the German Minister to Sweden, Hans Thomsen, and the representative of the German military attaché would leave for the Swedish-Norwegian frontier in order to inform the German commander in Norway, General Franz Böhme, of the situation. These two gentlemen took off from Barkarby airfield near Stockholm at 6.30 P.M. in a Swedish military plane.

The following day, May 6th, Thomsen reported that he had been met at the frontier in the morning by a representative of General Böhme.

Foreign Minister Joachim von Ribbentrop

Count Bernadotte's Red Cross car at Schönhausen

Count Bernadotte taking shelter during an air attack

This officer had informed him that Böhme was unwilling to capitulate with his forces unless he were to receive a direct order from Dönitz. He said that the German forces in Norway were quite intact and would be able to hold out without difficulty for a couple of months longer. He was therefore not prepared to act on an order to surrender issued by Envoy Schellenberg.

Immediately afterwards a telephone communication was received from Count Schwerin von Krosigk, who, it was reported, was at Mürwick together with the other members of the government. The Minister for Foreign Affairs gave the information that direct contact had been set up between the German Government and General Eisenhower, and that negotiations regarding Norway had been begun. Later in the day Schellenberg succeeded in getting into telephonic communication with Dönitz. He informed the Grand Admiral that apparently General Böhme had not been kept informed of the actual situation, and asked him to transmit a direct order that the capitulation in Norway be carried out. Dönitz replied that he might conceivably open direct negotiations with Eisenhower on this question, and that it was therefore not certain that the Swedish Government's assistance would be needed from then on.

At 10.15 on Monday, May 7th, came the final communication from Count Schwerin von Krosigk. In the night of May 6th–7th, the German Minister for Foreign Affairs reported that Germany's complete capitulation had been decided upon. Negotiations between him and General Eisenhower about the signing of the capitulation were still proceeding. I at once informed the Swedish Crown Prince, General C. A. Ehrensvärd of the Defense Staff, and Mr. Boheman of what had happened. I was probably the first Swede to learn of this great event.

This, then, was the end. The war in Europe was a thing of the past. The nightmare that was the Nazi system had ceased to be a reality. Millions of people could now set their minds on the work of reconstruction, the creation of a happier world. In this moment I felt profound gratitude that I had been privileged to take a part in the events of the final act, and perhaps thereby to have helped bring about an earlier armistice than might otherwise have been achieved. I had been given an opportunity to follow events of world history from close range. The curtain had now descended upon a world that had been through more evil and suffering, perhaps, than any earlier generation in the history of Europe.

EPILOGUE

In the course of my travels in Germany in the spring of 1945 I received much information about the leading figures of the Third Reich from sources that must be regarded as reliable. This information has convinced me that it is extremely important for the future well-being of the world that absolute clarity be attained on two points. First, it must be made absolutely clear to the German people that Germany in 1945 suffered a complete defeat, not only on the military front, but on all fronts, just as in 1918, when, however, German propaganda soon produced the "stab in the back" by the home front as the real reason for the defeat. The myth of German invincibility must once and for all be destroyed. No more legends such as the "stab in the back" must be countenanced. Secondly, the German people must be brought to see what kind of men the leaders of the Third Reich were. My experience tells me that they were men completely lacking in moral conceptions and human stature. In the final act there they were, with their hideous pasts, desperately intriguing among themselves, yet at the same time endeavoring to take shelter behind each other's backs, cowardly, undecided, irresolute. The final act of the drama of the Third Reich lacked any dignity or tragic quality. It was merely ignominious, because all the dramatis personæ were themselves ignominious and petty. They were not fighting for an ideal, a belief, a conviction: they were fighting merely for their lives, besmirched with crimes that could never be expiated.

Let us glance briefly at the leading figures of the Third Reich as they appeared in its thirteenth and last year. Take first the Führer. Already Grand Admiral Dönitz has introduced the legend that the Führer died the death of a hero, fighting for his people on the Occident's last barricades against upsurging Bolshevism. We shall see that in the best-informed German quarters a quite different opinion is held. The Führer did not die like a hero: it can be considered quite certain that he was murdered. True, he kept his leadership until the very last days of the Third Reich. But he had long lost the capacity for initiative. All he could do was to veto decisions made by his lieutenants. To his entourage he had become a figure of terror in almost the same degree as to the world at large. If anyone displeased him, he immediately had an order for execution prepared. At this final stage Adolf Hitler was physically and psychologically a branded man, in all probability marked by the disease that provides a tenable explanation of his insane acts and ideas. His hands shook; he could no longer walk; he could cross a room only with difficulty. He felt that the sands of his life were running out, and he was more than conscious of complete failure—of enemies about to corner him, of a situation more and more desperate. To the very last he kept telephoning to Himmler, roaring out his accusations in a desperate attempt to conjure up a change in the situation.

In Hitler's immediate entourage there was, in the first place, Eva Braun, his mistress. Eva Braun, who came of a Munich family and is said to have been a very beautiful woman, had, I have been told, a very great direct influence over Hitler. Altogether, her influence was considerable. It was she who, for example, paved the way for Obergruppenführer Kaltenbrunner, one of the most evil spirits among the little group of men and women who guided Germany's destiny in those days. Kaltenbrunner was an intimate friend of another member of the set, Gruppenführer Fegelein, who was married to a sister of Eva Braun. He advanced rapidly from being a humble riding master to the highest honors. These four—the two sisters Braun, Kaltenbrunner, and Fegelein—were among the most dangerous in the circle surrounding Hitler. In the final phase Kaltenbrunner spent several hours every day with the Führer and did all he could to work him up to continue the course upon which he had embarked so long ago.

Among the principal actors of the Third Reich in the finale was Reichsleiter Martin Bormann, the successor of Rudolf Hess, a man who also had a very great influence over Hitler. He specialized in intrigue, but he also possessed another talent that he found very useful: the ability to reduce complicated matters to the simplest terms in his reports to Hitler—a knack that the Führer warmly appreciated.

Goebbels, who drew strength from his own speeches, never ceasing to be fascinated by them even after practically everybody had ceased to believe what he said, and who from his safe shelter issued fiery orations exhorting the populace of Berlin to fight to the last man; Göring, who, according to what one hears, could never after 1940 be shaken in his belief that Germany had decisively won the war, and who in this belief allowed the Luftwaffe rapidly to deteriorate; Ribbentrop, with his stupid conceit and narrow outlook—all these belonged to the inner circle of those near Hitler at the last. Göring seems, however, to have ceased to have any influence.

And then there was Heinrich Himmler. Of him, one can only remark that he appears to have been quite as terrified of Hitler as Hitler was of him. The intimate circle around Hitler directed all their plottings specifically against the head of the Gestapo. As a result he was sent to the front;

at first, in the late autumn of 1944, to the Western front, and presently to the Oder front—the latter one of the most dangerous and exposed sectors. The assumption was that Himmler would fail there. He was to be first discredited, then liquidated.

Himmler ended as a suicide, but not before Hitler himself had been liquidated.

Shortly after the curtain had gone down on the drama of the European war, I had a long conversation with Schellenberg, who, as I have already related, had come to Stockholm to arrange the surrender of the German troops in Norway, and who still remained in the Swedish capital. My earlier dealings with Schellenberg had made it necessary for me to have a final conference with him. By reason of his opposition to the official policy he had felt constrained to support my plans in connection with the Red Cross. And it can be stated that the manner in which he exerted his influence at the end contributed in no small degree to sparing Denmark and Norway the horrors of destructive fighting. The decision that the German troops should surrender unconditionally was largely due to his energetic insistence.

Now Schellenberg was sitting with me telling of his own experience during the closing phase. He also gave me an insight into what had gone on behind the scenes in connection with my appearance on the German stage. His account, for the accuracy of which he himself must be responsible, appeared to me, from the point of view of history and as supplementing my own impressions, to possess so great an interest that its main points ought to be given publicity.

Schellenberg's Story

To begin with (Schellenberg said), I should like to hark back to a period of great significance. In 1943 Switzerland suddenly appeared in the very foreground of the political interests of the Reich. An attack on Switzerland very nearly took place. The plans had been prepared and approved by Ribbentrop and Bormann, and the military-political situation produced by the Allied landing in Italy seemed to have made such an attack necessary. I opposed these plans tooth and nail, partly by attempting to make contact with certain friends of mine in Switzerland. The idea was finally abandoned, mainly because of economic considerations. But Switzerland came very near to sharing the fate of Denmark and Norway and all the other occupied countries. The whole episode was very typical of the foreign policy of the Third Reich.

This was only one of the occasions on which I attempted actively to oppose the official policy. After I had become head of the Political Department of the German Intelligence Service and, in 1944, head of the whole organization, the defects of the regime became evident to me. The upper stratum was corrupt through and through. In my opinion the one exception was the head of the SS, Himmler. As the conviction grew in me that the policy directed by Hitler and Ribbentrop was bound to have catastrophic results, it became clear to me that it was a matter of life and death for Germany that a counterbalance to it be created. It was my belief that the only one who could create it was Himmler. It was in this spirit that I attempted to approach him and to obtain such an influence over him that his power would be turned in the desired direction. It was my conviction that Germany must in one way or another disengage itself from the war with the Western powers.

However strange it may sound, there was at the time of my appointment no real political intelligence service in the Third Reich. And there was even less understanding of its importance. It was regarded as superfluous for the simple reason that the Third Reich did not require information about the internal situation in other countries; the Third Reich could do without that. This opinion was shared by Hitler, who was completely opposed to me on this subject, as was also Ribbentrop. The only one who showed some interest was Himmler. But even he created difficulties for me, enslaved as he was by the prejudices created by the basic ideas of National Socialism, as well as by his own tendency to estimate political events with the mentality of a police official. It was only by slow degrees that I was able to bring about a change in his attitude.

As the military and political situation became more critical my position became more difficult. I became the object of special notice and interest on the part of the Gestapo and the Security Police. My most active and dangerous enemies were Reichsleiter Bormann and the head of the Security Police, Kaltenbrunner. In regard to Kaltenbrunner especially, I had to show great caution. As far back as eighteen months earlier he stated that he had complete evidence of my being employed by the [British] Secret Service. He did everything in his power to trap me.

This was the situation when, at the beginning of February, the German Minister in Stockholm, Thomsen, reported that you were about to start for Berlin in order to see Himmler. Twice that day Ribbentrop sent Geheimrat Wagner, his personal secretary in the Ministry for Foreign Affairs, to see me in order to try to find out if it was I who, through my personal connections in Sweden, had taken the initiative in arranging your mission. Ribbentrop and Kaltenbrunner regarded me as responsible for the pardon and liberation of the seven so-called Warsaw Swedes,[1] and they tried to show that my intervention in this case, especially in view of the hostility of the Swedish press towards Germany, was a great political blunder. In a general way they did everything they could to inflame Hitler's antipathy to Sweden, particularly by giving him reports about the training of Norwegian policemen in Sweden.

I told Wagner, what was the truth, that I had no knowledge of your projected visit, and I informed Himmler as well as Kaltenbrunner about these conversations. Himmler was interested, but also annoyed that the arrangements for your journey should have gone through the Legation in Stockholm, and consequently through the Ministry for

[1] Seven Swedes, including the Swedish Consul General and representatives of the L. M. Ericsson and Swedish Match companies, were arrested by the Germans in Poland in the late summer of 1942. It took two and a half years of continuous effort to get them released. TRANSLATOR

Foreign Affairs. This meant that he must treat your visit as being of an official nature and report it to Hitler. He therefore instructed Kaltenbrunner to make use of a favorable opportunity to mention the matter to Hitler and try to ascertain what his feelings were. Instead Kaltenbrunner asked Gruppenführer Fegelein to attend to the matter, and the following day Fegelein was in a position to report that the Führer was definitely opposed to the project. "Buffoonery of that sort won't help us in this war," was Hitler's comment.

And then you arrived in Berlin. I at once telephoned to Himmler, begged him earnestly not to ignore this gesture on the part of Sweden, and said that he absolutely must receive you. After a great many objections Himmler agreed that Kaltenbrunner should speak to Ribbentrop and I to Geheimrat Wagner and try to arrange for Ribbentrop to see you without Hitler's knowledge, and without letting Ribbentrop know that the Führer had forbidden your reception. If Ribbentrop agreed, then I and Kaltenbrunner could also see you, and in this way Himmler would gain time and see how things developed.

That is how it came about that Kaltenbrunner and I were able to see you. From the very beginning I had a feeling that I had made a useful contact. I saw in your visit the last opportunity of realizing what had always been at the back of my mind: in some way or other to steer Germany out of the war. I also made up my mind that a meeting between you and Himmler had to be arranged, and as soon as you left me I set about it in the following manner:

I complimented Kaltenbrunner on the remarkable way in which he had conducted his conversation with you—a perfect example of Austrian "ballroom diplomacy." There was something that I had long wanted to say to him, and I had now decided to bring it up in the course of my next meeting with Himmler. It was this: that in the present desperate situation Ribbentrop must be removed and Kaltenbrunner appointed Minister for Foreign Affairs in his place. Kaltenbrunner swallowed the bait so readily and with such enthusiasm that I found it difficult to control the situation. When, after that, we telephoned to Himmler, Kaltenbrunner insisted with burning conviction on the importance of your meeting him, even though Hitler had definitely forbidden it. When your meeting took place Kaltenbrunner was not asked to attend, and that made him furious. He sobered down, and soon he was showing himself to be as hostile to me as ever. After your first meeting with Himmler the intrigues began again. Kaltenbrunner heaped reproaches on me because I had made the Reichsleiter altogether too well disposed to you, and he enlisted the services of Gruppenführer Müller, the brutal administrative chief of the Gestapo, who made every kind of objection to the plan to collect the Norwegian and Danish prisoners in Neuengamme. Among other objections he said that the German population, especially the long trains of refugees, must not be exposed to the sight of Swedish Red Cross cars driving about the roads at night with prisoners from the concentration camps. I, however, would not give in, but visited

Himmler at his headquarters and had it out with him. I told him it was evident that Germany was about to collapse, and that in this situation he must on no account fail to make the most of your presence in Germany. I said that he must try to act independently in order to steer the German wreck into a peaceful haven before it capsized, and I suggested that he ask you to fly to General Eisenhower and present to him an offer of surrender. The talk became more and more emotional as it went on. I said that Himmler's proper place was in Berlin and not with an army group, that this was the second time that Hitler's entourage had succeeded in getting him away from the capital, and I told him that he should return there as soon as possible to prepare for peace, with or without using force. At last Himmler gave way. And that night I received very wide powers to negotiate with you. However, the next morning he rang me up, took back most of what he had said, and authorized me only to maintain contact with you and in certain circumstances to try to persuade you to see Eisenhower on your own initiative. From that day—it was at the beginning of March—there was a daily tug of war between Himmler and me, although neither Kaltenbrunner nor any other of the persons in Hitler's entourage was really aware of it.

In long talks with Himmler I tried to show him that it was no longer a question of being true to his oath to Hitler—who, as he himself always maintained, was the real basis of the SS organization—but a matter of life or death for the German people. His reply was always: "Then what you want me to do is to eliminate the Führer?" There was a time when I couldn't answer this question in the affirmative, for to have done so would have been to run the risk of being liquidated. That was because the influence possessed by Gruppenführer Fegelein, Obergruppenführer Kaltenbrunner, Obersturmbannführer Skorzeny the chief of the Werewolves, and others of their kind was so great, especially as it rested principally on their right to report personally to Hitler.

During these talks Himmler often spoke to me about the state of Hitler's health, which according to him was becoming worse from day to day. When I asked him how it was that Hitler still possessed such power, Himmler said that his energy continued undiminished. His abnormal way of life, his habit of turning night into day and only sleeping two or three hours, his restless activity and his continual outbursts of rage completely exhausted those near him and made the whole atmosphere unbearable. I suggested that the attempt on his life of July 20th may have seriously affected his health, particularly the injuries to his head, and Himmler thought this possible, but he pointed out the significance of Hitler's stooping more and more, his slack appearance, and the marked tremor in his left arm.

It was on the basis of these reports—personally I had not seen Hitler for a long time—that at the beginning of April I consulted a friend of mine, Professor de Crinis, Head of the Psychiatric Section of the Charité Hospital. In answer to my question he replied that he had observed in photographs in illustrated papers that Hitler's movements appeared almost paralyzed, and that he must regard this as a symptom of Parkinson's disease (paralysis agitans). I thereupon arranged a meeting between Himmler and de Crinis, to which the Reichsleiter summoned the Reichsminister of Health, Conti. It was evident that Himmler was extremely interested by what he heard.

A few days later—it was on April 13th—Himmler summoned me to his headquarters in Wustrow and took me for a walk in the forest, where he at last completely unburdened himself to me. "Schellenberg," he said, "I don't think that we can let the Führer go on any longer. Do you believe that de Crinis was right?" I answered: "Yes. True, it is two or three years since I have met Hitler, but judging by what I can gather about his recent behavior, I am convinced that it is high time for you to act."

But after a while Himmler's vacillations began again. It was clear that the breach between him and Hitler had begun. Over and over he asked me what he could do. He said that after all he could not murder the Führer. He could not give him poison, nor could he arrest him in the Reich

Chancellery, for in that event the whole military machine would come to a stop. I replied that this would not matter. There was only one way out. He must present himself before Hitler, inform him of everything that had happened recently, and force him to abdicate. Himmler said that this was absolutely impossible: the Führer would burst into a rage and shoot him on the spot. "You must take suitable precautions to prevent that," I said. "After all, you have a sufficient number of SS men in high positions who are capable of arranging an arrest of this kind. If there is no other way we must get the doctors to help."

Our walk lasted an hour and a half. Himmler was not able to come to a decision. He said only that he would arrange a meeting of Professor de Crinis, Professor Morell, Hitler's personal physician, Doctor Stumpfegger, his second physician, and Bormann.

A couple of days later I asked Professor de Crinis what conclusion he and his colleagues had reached. He answered rather disappointedly that he had discussed with Doctor Stumpfegger principally the supposed symptoms of Parkinson's disease. Stumpfegger had not shared his opinion, although he had to accept some of his points. In the end they had agreed on certain medicines, which he had prepared in his clinic; but Stumpfegger had not called for them, having himself had the intention of procuring medicines. There was therefore a possibility that Stumpfegger had no intention of getting the medicines in de Crinis' clinic. I reported this to Himmler, and he begged me insistently to keep the whole business to myself.

During the days following my walk with Himmler on April 13th events began to move in the direction I had long anticipated. During the first week in April I had got into touch with Count Schwerin von Krosigk, who was then Minister of Finance. In the course of long talks we agreed that the war must be brought to an end in order to save as much of Germany as possible. In connection with these talks I arranged a meeting for April 19th between Himmler and von Krosigk. Relations between these two men had been broken off for a long time.

Before the meeting Himmler was extremely strung up, and at the last moment he wanted to cancel it. However, it took place in the presence of Reichsarbeitsminister Seldte, who had at one time been the leader of the Stahlhelm. During the meeting von Krosigk talked with Himmler while I conferred with Seldte. The latter was of the opinion that Himmler must take over the leadership and compel Hitler, on the occasion of his birthday, to read a proclamation to the German people in which it should be announced that a plebiscite would be held, a new party formed, and the People's Courts abolished.

After the conference von Krosigk informed me that he had discussed with Himmler all the questions that we had gone over, and that he had earnestly entreated him to take action against the Führer. Himmler thanked me for having arranged a meeting with the Minister of Finance. I replied that in my opinion von Krosigk was the only person whom he could appoint as Ribbentrop's successor in the Ministry for Foreign Affairs. Himmler agreed with me; but then he began to speak about the Allies' propaganda against himself in connection with the concentration camps. "The whole thing is senseless. It won't in any case make any difference to me, but you must not believe this propaganda. It isn't true."

I cannot describe in detail the events of the following days. Hitler's birthday passed without event. On April 21st you had another meeting with Himmler. During this time Himmler was complaining to me that his health was not any too good, and I noticed how nervous and strained he was. "Schellenberg," he said to me on one occasion, "I am filled with horror at the thought of what is now coming." Another time he told me what he would do when power was in his hands. He requested me the same evening to propose a name for the new party that it had been suggested he found. I proposed "Party of National Unity." Himmler then took up the question of the liquidation of Hitler, but only in vaguely allusive terms.

On the night of April 23rd–24th there was another meeting between you and Himmler in

Lübeck, at which he asked you to present an offer of surrender to the Western powers, to be transmitted through the Swedish Government. It was then that he said it could only be "a question of one, two, or at most three days before the Führer ends his dynamic life in this dramatic struggle."

According to my calculations the life of the Führer ended on April 27th, and it is my definite belief that it was by means of an injection. However, I do not know who it was that administered it to him.

The events in Berlin on the following day, April 28th, are probably not generally known. It is certain, however, that Grand Admiral Dönitz's nomination as Hitler's successor took place on the 29th. There are also fairly certain grounds for believing that it was Reichsleiter Bormann who made the nomination. It was the last move against Himmler. Himmler realized that capitulation was unavoidable, and that for this reason he had been pushed aside.

Meanwhile I was continuing my negotiations

with you and with Himmler. My endeavors were in the first place to bring about a peaceful solution of the Danish and Norwegian problem, in order that Germany might not further burden herself with the senseless destruction of the Scandinavian countries. On April 29th I accompanied you to Copenhagen to negotiate with, among others, Doctor Best, and then, as you know, I immediately returned to Germany. When I arrived at the place where Himmler was I was informed that not he, but Dönitz, had been nominated Hitler's successor, and that that same night the first conference between Himmler and Dönitz had taken place at Plön, in Holstein, and that the Reichsleiter, in accordance with my earlier proposal, had succeeded in obtaining the nomination of Schwerin von Krosigk as Ribbentrop's successor. Himmler was very much depressed, for in the army, too, there was no real appreciation or understanding of his struggle to obtain an agreement with the Western powers about capitulation. Himmler was now considering whether he should resign and commit suicide, but he wanted to discuss the situation once more with me.

Some hectic and nerve-racking days followed, without sleep and with difficult and dangerous motor drives through the actual battle zone. When, on May 1st, I first arrived with Himmler at Dönitz's headquarters at Plön, I found a very tense atmosphere. It was soon evident that von Krosigk held the same views as Himmler and I, whereas Dönitz, as well as Keitel and Jodl—that is, the chief military commanders—were not at that time in any circumstances prepared to give up Norway without a fight. They particularly pointed out that the German commander in Norway, Colonel General Böhme, was in a very strong strategic position.

The negotiations continued. For a long time Dönitz hesitated to agree to the proposals of von Krosigk and myself. In the end I was appointed envoy, with instructions to conduct negotiations in Stockholm for the surrender of the troops in Norway. As for the events from then until May 7th, they are known to you.

Thus far Schellenberg. As I listened to him, countless impressions of the months just past flashed through my mind. I had received further confirmation of the opinion I expressed on my return home from one of my last trips to Germany. I said at that time: "I return to Sweden an even firmer opponent of the Nazi creed than before, but at the same time I cannot help having a deep sympathy for Germany's unhappy people." They have been found wanting. They have allowed themselves to be led by ruthless scoundrels. They must drain the cup of suffering. But as the representative of an organization with the humanitarian spirit of the Red Cross, I must urge that afterwards they be helped and led in other paths, not with hatred and brutality, but by those who understand that love for humanity is the strongest of all forces for good. Then, and then only, can we look to see the downfall of the Third Reich followed by a happier scheme of things for cruelly tried humanity.

PRINTER'S NOTE

THIS book was set on the Linotype in Janson, a recutting made direct from the type cast from matrices made by Anton Janson some time between 1660 and 1687.

Of Janson's origin nothing is known. He may have been a relative of Justus Janson, a printer of Danish birth who practised in Leipzig from 1614 to 1635. Some time between 1657 and 1668 Anton Janson, a punch-cutter and type-founder, bought from the Leipzig printer Johann Erich Hahn the type-foundry which had formerly been a part of the printing house of M. Friedrich Lankisch. Janson's types were first shown in a specimen sheet issued at Leipzig about 1675.

Composed, printed, and bound by H. Wolff, New York. Typography by James Hendrickson.